Congratulations,
Enjoy the ride
Happy Travels
best,
Edward

The Destination Diaries:
How to Travel for Life

By Edward P. Dramberger, PhD "The Destination Dr."

DORRANCE
PUBLISHING CO
EST. 1920
PITTSBURGH, PENNSYLVANIA 15238

Dorrance Publishing Co
585 Alpha Drive
Suite 103
Pittsburgh, PA 15238
Visit our website at *www.dorrancebookstore.com*

ISBN: 978-1-4809-6030-5
eISBN: 978-1-4809-6053-4

To my parents and family for instilling the belief that anything was possible.

And to my friends, colleagues, and fellow travelers for making everything possible.

"We travel not to escape life, but for life not to escape us."
-unknown

Contents

Author's Note

This is a work of non-fiction. Everything in these stories happened as described except where some names, locations, and dates have been changed to protect the privacy of those involved.

Prologue: Travel is the Best Medicine

Before I traveled to 180 different countries, lived on six continents, and enjoyed a rewarding career in Hospitality & Tourism, I was depressed. As a graduate student living in Virginia, I had let enough consecutive bad days stack up without a semblance of light at the end of the tunnel. I trapped myself in the house for as long as I could bare until enough was enough and I decided to go see the university counselor.

He ran some tests. I answered some questions. Afterward, he asked if I would be willing to see a psychiatrist. Nothing else had worked, so I agreed and visited one the very same day. Through the course of a few meetings, the psychiatrist diagnosed me with bipolar I disorder.

My doctor helped me understand the difference between the two branches of the disorder. We discussed the common behavior associated. Although I'd never had a manic episode, he described how they usually played out.

"Drugs, sex, crime," he said. "Any or all these behaviors could arise when someone is in a manic state."

It was news to me. I had been healthy throughout my life. Nothing out of the psychological ordinary existed in my family. I confided in him that I was afraid.

"Is there a medication I need to be on or some sort of advice you have for how to manage my disorder?" I asked.

"Let me ask you this," he said, skimming through the notes for my case file. "What makes you happy?"

"Travel," I blurted out without a moment's hesitation.

He paused and touched his pen to his chin.

"Well if it makes you happy and you don't get into trouble," he said. "Then do it."

For years, I'd felt guilty for deriving so much pleasure out of my trips. Whether they were domestic or international, rural or urban, travel was like a drug to me. I was relieved to discover that it was a cure, not a contraband.

"That's it?" I asked, like a child who just had his hands caught in the cookie jar. "Just, travel?"

"Yeah," he said simply. "Based on our conversations and everything in your file, travel is the best thing to prescribe to you."

The weeks leading up to my depressive streak, I had been preparing for a move to New York City, where I had just landed the first big gig of my career, set to start right after graduation. It was a huge deal. It was the type of job I always thought I wanted but I was hesitant. I would have to stay put in New York with minimal vacation time for at least 24 months.

"Okay," I said to the doctor, dumbfounded. "Great."

The doctor gave me permission to do what I really wanted to already: ditch the New York Job offer in favor of taking my chances abroad. There was uncertainty to be sure, but I suddenly felt a weight off my shoulders. My father always told me I wasn't happy unless I was traveling. It turns out, he was more correct than he ever imagined.

So, I left the doctor's office, and never looked back.

Part I: Connection

By foot, plane, train, and automobile — just as there are so many ways we travel, there are also so many reasons why we travel. Perhaps none of them are as common as our innate desire as human beings for connection with one another. We travel to connect with others for friendship, for business, for love. I'm no different.

My first travel memories take place in the back of a station wagon, sitting beside my twin brother on a bench of reverse-facing seats, watching the painted broken-line of the highway pass beneath us like a game of packman in rewind.

We took yearly road trips from our home in San Antonio to my maternal grandmother's house in Albuquerque. Our entire eight-person family would pack into the brown and beige boat of a Buick, with its wood-paneled siding, and make the slog across the desert. For ten hours, there was nothing to see apart from the paint on the highway, the tumble weeds, and the empty expanses.

Inevitably, with so many people to please and fights between siblings to mitigate, my parents decided it was necessary to break the drive into two legs. We would always stay in Fort Stockton, West Texas where it was truly hotter than hell in the summer time. My parents would choose between the Holiday Inn and the Howard Johnson, and the six of us kids would pour out of the vehicle like a pack of animals ready to prey on the place.

With the relentless heat, our first stop was always the pool. We'd jump in, splash around, and when we got out we didn't even need a towel to dry off.

If we waited five minutes, the sun was powerful enough to dry us completely. Even with their seemingly foolproof plan to let the kids expend their stored-up energies at the pool, my parents knew they had to monitor the situation for any additional mischief. Once, my younger sister, who was only four or five at the time, jumped in without a fear in the world to join in on our fun. The problem, of course, was she couldn't swim. My dad jumped in with his clothes on to save her before realizing she was fine just splashing in the water near the pool ladder.

It was interesting to watch my family operate outside the normal environments of home, school, work and regular extracurricular activities. The interactions were different than they were in those controlled environments. If my dad could suddenly jump into a pool with his clothes on, it seemed like anything was possible on the road. Certainly, I felt my connections with my family deepen — and sometimes divide — on these long drives, the way family road trips often go, but it was our stop at these roadside hotels where I made some of the more interesting connections of my young life.

From early on, I was delighted to see the unmistakable green of the Holiday Inns signs. It meant I would be treated to interactions with the hotel staff. Our family would get two rooms: one for the boys and one for my parents who let the little ones stay with them. The freedom afforded by the thin-walled separation meant my brothers and I would play games. Hide and seek was usually the favorite. Once, when it was my turn to hide, I thought it might make the game more exciting if we played in complete darkness. I took the room key and stuck it into the electric socket to short circuit the power in the whole hotel. I'd read something to that effect in a comic book and to my astonishment, it worked.

When the hotel night manager, a young pimply teenager, came to the door to ask what happened. My dad told him we had all just been sitting there. My little sister started crying out of embarrassment because my father was wearing only boxer shorts as he answered the door. The young man scanned the eight of us — we'd all huddled into my parents' room after things went dark — and splashed each of us with the flashlight. I wasn't the most mischievous child at home, but on the road doing things I wouldn't usually do felt, somehow, right. I enjoyed being someone other than my regular self. Since we gave nothing away, he shrugged and went to reset the breaker.

Later, at the hotel's restaurant for dinner, I tried on the personality of fine-diner. I ordered the most expensive thing on the menu — shrimp, baked potatoes, a rib-eye steak — while my siblings opted for burgers, fries, and pizza. I complained to the same hotel night manager about why the potato wasn't up to par. My parents just rolled their eyes. They, like my siblings, thought I was crazy for ordering these outlandish items in the first place. On the road, I was different. I expected service. Even at seven or eight years old, I felt I wanted to be waited on as a traveler and that desire led me to my first connection with someone in the service industry.

After dinner, I was bored trying to wait until I was tired enough to fall asleep. The soundtrack to my boredom was the dripping noises emanating from our room's toilet. I couldn't even be bored in peace, I thought to myself. So, I decided to wander down to the front desk and take it up with the staff.

"Excuse me sir," I said, before the night manager could even look up from his reservation log. "The toilet doesn't work."

He sighed, then asked, "Where are your parents?"

"My parents?" I answered. "Look, I am a guest at this hotel and this is a problem."

He looked at me for a moment before saying, "You seem like quite the experienced traveler."

"I am," I lied. Apart from these small road trips, I'd never traveled in my short-seven years of life. I did like to sit in the bathtub and take my treasured plastic globe, spin it around, and then point to a spot at random, declaring that one day I would visit.

The manager looked at me for a while, watching to see if I would flinch. When I didn't, he walked with me to the room. After he fixed the noisy toilet, he turned to me and whispered, "In the future, if you want to get on the good side of the hotel staff, you should always serve complaints in a compliment sandwich."

"A compliment sandwich?" I asked, trying not to raise my voice and wake my siblings.

"You say something nice about the hotel — maybe it has a beautiful painting or everything looks spotless — then you share your complaint," he explained. "After you're finished, you just wrap it up with another compliment to leave them feeling good."

I pondered this for a moment then asked, "Does it work?"

"A lot better than you'd think," he said, patting my head. "Besides, not all the hotel staffers are going to think you're as endearing as I do."

He walked down the hall and I went to bed, feeling like I learned a valuable lesson I likely never would have at school in San Antonio.

When we finally arrived in New Mexico the next day, we were all jittery about getting to see my maternal grandfather. He was well off. He used to line us up — my two older brothers first, then my twin brother and I, then my younger brother, and younger sister — then he would give us money according to our age. We thought it was the coolest thing, every year we got a little more than the year before. We'd take the money and spend it on trinkets from the Native Americans in town or buy ice cream on the way back from Carlsbad Caverns, which were just about the only cool place to visit in the summer time.

He had a farm with my grandmother outside of Albuquerque. There were goats, chickens, and cows. My grandfather had hired a young Hispanic man to help with the farm. He was tall and thin, but the type of scruffy guy that's helpful around a farm. He treated us kids well. He showed us how to feed hay to the goats and cows. Once, when the farm flooded the whole valley, he braved the storm and helped not just my grandfather but the nearby farmers too. I felt a warm connection with him, a friend away from home.

He asked a few of the boys if we wanted to help him out one day. Normally, I wasn't a fan of farm work. My grandfather had asked us to do things in the past and I always found a way to sneak out of it. Yet, when my friend — this man who helped my grandfather — would ask me, I was all for it. The task at hand was a trip down to the local grocery store where they had arranged to take the produce that was no longer fresh enough to be left out for shoppers and bring it back to feed the animals. We piled into the back of the pickup truck and off we went.

What would have normally been a gross experience — salvaging old, stinky produce — became fun. My connection with the hired help made me feel somehow important and useful. I had a function. In a small way, the activity itself made my summer more meaningful than it would have been otherwise. On the way home, we brothers even got to have a mini food-fight, tossing gooey tomatoes at each other in the bed of the pickup truck.

Although I enjoyed the money, the short trips we took, and the adventures in the back of the truck, when I could, I chose to spend the sweltering afternoons in Albuquerque indoors. I'd turn on the television and watch a show about how young kids lived in Europe or follow Johnny Quest on his fantastic, worldwide adventures. When the TV was occupied, I would look at the pictures in National Geographic magazine.

One afternoon, my uncle, who had served as a paratrooper in wars abroad was watching one of the shows with me when my mother came in.

"Edward, why don't you go out and play?" she asked.

"I went to the zoo yesterday," I said, hoping to finish the episode of the show about the lives of European kids. "Can I stay?"

"That's good you're watching this," she said, looking at the TV. Usually my other siblings chose to watch cartoons, which in my parents' view, had a far lower educational value. "But you need to go out and play,"

I rose to my feet slowly and got ready to go outside.

"Oh, come on," my uncle spoke up. "Let the boy learn about the world."

Just then, even though the travel was taking place on the televisions screen, I realized the capacity for it to bring people together. My uncle and I hardly knew each other, we rarely spoke, and yet, there in my grandfather's living room, it was clear we shared a passion for travel that made us different than the other members of our family.

My early family road trips taught me how much easier it is to get connected with others when you travel. It's because you can be anybody you want to be. You can be as honest or as dishonest as you want. The lines between truth and lies are blurred. You can say whatever you want. You can do things you wouldn't usually do.

For traveling, you must go in with an open mind. Not all the experiences are good experiences, but I do know this much: locals will be just as interested in you as you are in them, how you live, how you make a living, what interests you in life, or why do you do the things that you do. Although I cultivated my ability to connect with different kinds of people in this way, from those early road trips, I've never felt too much like an outsider. I can sleep on the bench at the train station or stay in the Ritz Carleton in back-to-back nights without batting an eye.

The weird thing in 21ˢᵗ century travel, is that you can travel for four days from the Chicagos and New Yorks of the world, to the most remote places on earth, then four or five days back. Transporting yourself to a place where they eat differently, their language is different, and their customs are different, can be a jarring experience. You may not even be able to have a conversation with the locals because they don't understand more than just your language. Just as a rich guy from a Saudi Royal family might not be able to conceive of your reality travel wise, the opposite person in the streets of Manila may not be able to fathom how easily you move about the world. Nobody intimidates me, not a rich person, not a poor person, and travel is the lubricant that sets you free from ignorance and gives you freedom to connect.

A Lobby in São Paulo

The condensation on my beer bottle has soaked through the label. I slide my thumb across it, sending droplets away and revealing the letters: S, K, O, L. Skol, or *Shhkol*, as the Paulistas pronounce it, is the beer I've seen most in my many trips to Brazil and this time is no different. As I glance around the cocktail lounge, most of the conference attendees — at least the Brazilians — clutch their own bottles of Skol snuggly in their palms as they circle the room. Others hold high-ball glasses or thin-stemmed martinis. A few of my fellow gringo colleagues opt for imported beers like Heineken or Stella Artois.

This is a scene I know well: name tags, tailored suits, big smiles, and libations. It's an effective recipe for connection-making across the world. For many, travel is synonymous with business. The modern era and technology has ushered in a new age where nearly all businesses aspire to be global. For these ambitious folks, booking flights and registering at conferences in cities like these are often a monthly or even weekly occurrence.

Throughout human history, people have been traveled to settlements and towns, villages and cities for the same purpose: business connections. Though, today's commercial hubs are much larger than our agrarian ancestors. In the United States of America, when we think of big cities a few come to mind: New York, Los Angeles, Chicago. For those, like me, who grow up in Texas, we might even throw Houston in for good measure. Though these cities are world famous to many outside our borders, they are far from massive by global standards. Shanghai, Tokyo, and Lagos dwarf their U.S. counterparts. In fact, of the four largest American metropolises I mentioned above, only New York makes it on the list of the worlds' 25 most populous cities. The Big Apple isn't even the largest city in the Americas — that distinction belongs to São Paulo.

With over twelve million inhabitants, Brazil's largest city is indeed a megacity. Like its counterparts in other emerging economies in China, India, Nigeria, and Indonesia, São Paulo is an almost incalculably complex place. That makes it a hive for connection, business and otherwise.

I take a swig of my beer and start to make my rounds. There are a few familiar faces from conferences in the past. I strike up a conversation with two of them — Bill and Dawn — about their respective visits to Brazil thus far.

Bill spent the week prior in Rio de Janiero, soaking up the sands at Ipanema beach and guzzling down a few Caipirinhas. It's his first time to the country so he wanted to take advantage. I certainly didn't object.

"Picanha," Dawn says, almost drooling as she summarized the succulent cut of Brazilian sirloin that has long charmed meat loving visitors. As a Texan, here was someone speaking to my heart. We raise our cattle proudly in the Longhorn State, but Brazil boasted some of the best beef out there: the sirloin cap, or rump cover, known as picanha is considered the most prized selection by locals.

The three of us get on well, as we have at other tourism conferences. We continue our conversation as the fried finger food — *coxinhas* and *pao de queijo* — begin to circulate. Between plates of savory delights, I spot a pair of young Brazilians couples eyeballing our small circle. Ice breakers at any conference can be challenging for people who aren't familiar with them, but language barriers make it all the more difficult.

"*Tudo bom?*" I ask them, exhausting most of my Brazilian Portuguese skills in the introductory phrase. The young couples — two men and two women — grin and approach us. I introduce them to Bill and Dawn. We all clink our beverages in celebration of our being newly connected.

The more we talk, the more it became apparent these two young couples have no idea what they were doing here. They made vague allusions to hotels they either owned or wanted to own. When asked if they plan to visit any of the panels the next day, they look at each other with blank expressions. Then, after having a small conference of their own in Portuguese, one calling himself João, awkwardly asks us if we had spare cash to get one of the girls a taxi home.

It certainly wasn't the first time I've been asked for money in my travels but those requesting money don't often wear suits and inquire at a conference cocktail hour.

Bill, whispering in my ear, says, "I don't know, these guys seem like con artists to me."

Dawn overhearing his comment, nods slightly in my direction.

I concede the toast may have been a bit premature — we certainly weren't going to make any substantial business deals with these four — but I feel strongly that everyone deserves the benefit of the doubt until they prove otherwise.

"How much do you need?" I ask, ignoring Bill and Dawn as they clear their throats.

"Fifty Reis," João said.

I reached into my wallet and hand him 60 Brazilian Real, the equivalent of $20, all in good faith. He tells me to meet him in twenty minutes, downstairs in the lobby. He explains he will send the woman home then run to the nearest ATM to pay me back. I nod and they leave.

As soon as they are out of earshot, Bill and Dawn let me have it.

"You idiot," Bill says.

"That's the oldest trick in the book," Dawn adds.

"Don't get duped Dramberger," Bill warns. "These folks are just after money."

I listen to their complaints. They remind me of where I am — in a developing country. They remind me of who I am — a white man from a developed country. To them, the math is simple and I have made a big mistake.

"Maybe," I shrug.

We change the subject, eat a few more snacks, I finish my beer and excuse myself. As I walk across the marble floors toward the elevator shafts, I think about Bill and Dawn's attitudes. It brought to mind the last time I was in São Paulo.

I'd gone to a nightclub alone, looking for some entertainment. Through the course of the evening, I met a couple wealthy local guys and gals. They had shown me a great time that night, treating me to drinks, and even buying me a late-night meal when we left the club.

If I'd been cagey or fearful about their intentions, I would have never met them or enjoyed their company. Nor would they have enjoyed mine. We would have missed the connection.

As I ride the elevator down to the lobby, I realize this is what I loved about megacities — the mystery. They excite me. The energies in these cities are like newly purchased battery packs for me, charging me up for weeks after I leave them behind. I get lost in them and I love it.

When the elevator dings open, straight ahead are the spinning doors of the main entrance. Even as the night wears on, the lobby was a flurry of activity. There are all kinds of people rushing around.

I watch all the different business men shuffle in and out. Some look frustrated. Others are intoxicated, maybe deals had been struck or mergers confirmed. I imagine the jungle of concrete and glass through the doors past them, where the haves tell their Mercedes drivers to turn and the have-nots sell trinkets on the streets to make enough for a small dinner.

I take a seat on a leather chair, angled toward the doorway. Besides the business people, there are families: piling in with their kids three or four at a time. I watch the worn out faces of two parents as their twin boys punch and kick each other in their race past to the elevators, reminding me of my road trips with my brothers. I see a young mother pat her sleeping child on the back, grateful to be coming back to a clean bed but most happy her daughter is finally asleep.

I also notice an awkward young man escort a woman way out of his league. He taps his toes nervously waiting for the elevator to arrive and the woman cracks a grin. An older gentleman reads a newspaper on a chair adjacent to mine. The longer I sit and watch the people flow through the lobby, the more I forget why I came downstairs in the first place.

Megacity's have endless possibilities for connections. When one is missed, that only makes room for another one to happen. I watch the lobby and it puts me at ease the same way people talk about needing to have the TV on to fall asleep. The promise of a megacity is enough for me, even if I know it can occasionally lie.

When Bill and Dawn ask me if João ever came back with my money the next morning at breakfast, I tell them I'm grateful he hadn't.

A Hostel in Johannesburg

She was blonde. Her long legs seemed to stretch on to infinity. She would cross them in a rhythm that matched how she flipped through her guidebook in the hostel common room in Melville, a bohemian neighborhood not far from the downtown area of South Africa's capital city.

Hostels are hardly the first accommodation that comes to mind when you think of romance, at least not of the long-term variety. They are places for budget travelers. Even the better, cleaner hostels can carry a certain unkemptness that no amount of air freshener can mask. Still, they are venues for some of the most precious moments for connections in all the traveling world. If for no other reason than that conversation with fellow hostel dwellers can help you pass the time until you can move on to nicer digs.

He was also blonde. He walked into the common room the way an athlete might walk onto the court from the locker rooms before a big game. It was as though he'd be practicing for the moment his whole life, such was the warmth he brought into the room on the chilly summer evening. When the blonde girl glanced up to see him arrive and their eyes met, a palpable electricity permeated the air and it was not only metaphorical.

Johannesburg sits on The Highveld, an expansive plateau comprising 400,000 square kilometers in the center of the country. The city itself sits at about 1,750 meters above sea level. At the end of the year, when it's summer in the southern hemisphere, The Highveld produces some of the most spectacular lightning storms in the world, a fact my new friend Victoria told me, as the two of us watched the young blonde man speak to the blonde woman for the first time.

She and I were playing Jenga on a table nearby.

"The hairs on the back of your neck standing up yet Ed?" she joked.

"Not yet," I answered, sliding out a Jenga brick and setting it on the tower. "Are yours?"

"Yep, and not just because of the impending lightening," she said, taking a moment to examine our growing tower of wooden bricks.

I met Victoria in Soweto on my third day in town. I decided to visit the country's most famous township the day after I had visited the upscale, posh area called Sandton in the northern part of the city. There, I was taken to a fancy lunch at a casino by an old business acquaintance. It wasn't a miserable time by any means, but if wanted casinos and white table cloths, I could have gone to Vegas. I came to Johannesburg to see Soweto.

Soweto stands for South Western Townships and is a collection of communities outside Johannesburg. Formed in the early 1900s to combat the rise of the bubonic plague, residents of these communities tended to be less fortunate than elsewhere in the city and lived in incredibly poor conditions until the last few decades. Still, Soweto is the only place in the world that birthed two Nobel Prize winners in Nelson Mandela and Desmond Tutu.

Victoria was also from Soweto and served as my private tour guide for my first trip to the area. Through the course of our day visiting the sights, meeting the people, and learning about the history of the community, I also learned a great deal about Victoria. Born as a man, her original birth name had been Victor. She struggled a great deal with her gender identity and sexual orientation in Soweto's unforgiving streets.

Years earlier, she explained over a lunch of Bunny Chow — a curry bread bowl made for workers and a specialty of South Africa's seaside city Durban — she had found someone special. Victoria and her lover fell deeply. The two of them were inseparable. People in the community didn't approve of their partnership and both of their families disowned them. The two lovers sought comfort in each other and, eventually, in drugs after they both began working in the sex industry to pay for basic necessities.

Victoria's candidness struck a chord in me. I had only just met this woman and she had provided her life story with such a clarity and compassion that tears welled in my eyes as we finished the meal. As we lapped up the last of the savory orange curry with pieces of the soaked bread loaf, she revealed the last part of her love story: she lost her lover to violence after a financial dispute with an unknown client.

After a long silence, Victoria picked back up the conversation and explained how she'd decided to fully root herself in her female identity and found a job as a tour guide for Soweto with foreigners like me.

I had never met anyone like Victoria and we became fast friends. The next day, before our Jenga game, she had shown me around downtown Joberg, pointing out some of the areas where she'd frequented in the years running up to her tragedy and her decision to change her life. Many of these places were worse than anything I'd seen in Soweto: makeshift shelters, open and rampant drug use, feral animals. I was shocked. Victoria had seen more horrors in her short life than I could have imagined.

We dined that evening at an unassuming Nigerian restaurant in nearby Hillbrow. The oxtail stew was served with garri, a type of processed cassava, that you use to soak and scoop out the broth and ingredients in the delicious strew. It was over our second meal that Victoria and I conversed about the nature of love.

"Love," Victoia said summarizing her view. "Is all about science: opposites attracting and all that."

I countered that I didn't believe that was always the case, pointing to all the similarities between happy couples I knew.

"Well," she said after hearing my retort. "You might not see on the outside how two different people can be beneath their appearance."

The air grew heavy and Victoria warned that a storm was rolling in. We agreed to disagree about love and I invited her back to the hostel to continue the conversation over some board games. After we began to play Jenga and the all-blonde connection had been initiated, huge dark clouds rolled in, illuminated by the city lights.

I watched the storm build through an open window behind the blondes and whispered to Victoria that the two proved I was right about matches being more similar than different. They were surely both from Europe, I theorized, on holiday in South Africa for safari and just needed a place to crash for a night or two.

"Interesting theory," Victoria said, slyly. "But I think we need a closer look to be sure."

Despite all she'd been through, Victoria still believed in true love, the kind that could be felt more than it could be seen. To her love wasn't a guarantee. It wasn't promised to everyone. It was rare. Like lightening, it was frightening and dangerous but it was beautiful and even if the science says it will never strike twice, she wouldn't let odds rain on her parade. She had a sense for it like some people do storms.

"Whops," she said, deliberately pulling out the Jenga block that sent the tower tumbling to the floor. I helped her pick up the pieces, trying to hold in my laughter. The two blondes came over and helped us collect the blocks.

Victoria asked in a deadpan tone, "You guys want to play?"

We discovered during our game that the woman was from the Netherlands and the man was from Australia. They had never met but had both signed up to start volunteering with WWOOF (worldwide opportunities on organic farms) the following week. I'd been right about their having some similarities. She'd been correct about their coming from different places. It remained to be seen who was the more accurate.

Then, while the girl from Amsterdam contemplated her move during one of her turns, the Australian boy leaned over and whispered something in her ear. Her lips curled into the slightest smile as she reached forward and plucked a piece out of the tower. Whatever he'd said to her sent a charge through the room, not unlike what was going on outside. You could just feel it.

When the girl finally set the piece on top of the tower, I thought the whole world would collapse if it fell. The energy between them was that powerful. Victoria looked at me right then, the lightning storm providing a cracking soundtrack to our game, and grinned as wide as The Highveld.

An Airplane from Moscow

"Shhhh," I said as quietly as I could, reaching for the bundle of cotton and flesh the stewardess presented to me.

I grazed the arm of the passenger beside me with the bundle's tiny foot. He groaned, eyes hidden behind a sleep mask, and smashed his face further into the flimsy complimentary pillow, its cover like a dryer sheet. The air was stale, the way it gets when you're among a few hundred drowsy passengers, tens of thousands of feet off the ground. Most of them aboard the Boeing 747 were asleep or trying to be. Only a couple LED-screen-lit faces stood out in the crowd as I stood up with the bundle.

"There, there," I took the lump in my hands and began to sway the baby the way my mother had done to me as a child.

About twenty minutes earlier, I had squeezed out of my middle seat — usually the least desirable place for a 6' 1" body like mine — to go to the bathroom. While using the facilities, I heard a chorus of crying babies nearby. It wasn't the usual whining baby sound, it was as if someone was starting an a cappella group with cranky infants.

Once I was finished fiddling around in the tiny closet-like toilet space, I emerged to a group of air stewards and stewardesses crisscrossing in front of me with babies in their arms. The flight attendants were bickering in Russian. While I couldn't understand what they were saying, I didn't need a translator to realize they were in trouble.

Few places can be as awkward for making connections as the inside of an airplane on a transcontinental flight. Flying stresses people out. There are those who have developed outright flying phobias, needing heavy doses of medication to make it through the duration of a flight. Even for folks who travel more often, there is a heightening of neuroses where a certain food, seating arrangement, or entertainment option needs to be secured if they are going to feel at ease.

To make matters worse, international flights are full of people who are either exhausted after a long vacation, eager to start their holiday, or irritated that they are only traveling for business or familial emergencies while all these people around them are vacationing. This diversity of emotions makes sitting down on a plane a sort of connection roulette where you hope the person next to you can at least respect whatever state of mind you arrive in.

Usually, people want to be left unbothered. Most everyone's had an experience with a talkative passenger — whether they are speaking with you or engaging someone else in conversation nearby — where patience and kindness are put to the test. I always do my best to be cordial. On a few shorter flights, I've engaged in incredibly interesting conversations and made friends I'm proud to say I've kept to this day. However, there is always one thing that everyone seems to agree can make or break an in-flight experience: a crying baby.

During none of my hundreds of international flights had I ever come across so many crying infants in one place. It was as if the Moscow's Sheremetyevo International Airport staff had decided to place an entire day's worth of babies on one flight. There were so many of them the already-overworked flight attendants were now playing babysitter on top of their regular duties.

"Excuse me," I said. Two of the flight attendants stopped talking to each other and looked over at me like I'd just asked for a hot towel.

"Yes, sir," one said. "Can I help you?"

"Well, I was going to see if I could help you," I asked.

The two shared a puzzled glance, the babies wailing in their arms.

I had caught a few winks of sleep after the inflight meal, using my trusty ear-plugs. I felt rested. Besides, I wasn't eager to squeeze back into my middle seat if I could help it.

A passenger near the bathrooms cleared his throat the way you do when you don't have anything stuck there, but just want to let people around you know that you're not thrilled about something. That something was crying babies. Another passenger pressed the button for assistance. Slowly the sleeping masses of passengers were waking up and they weren't happy. The flight attendants had no choice.

One transferred the baby from her arm into mine as she dashed off to attend to the irked passenger. I looked down at the beanie-wearing child, and stared at his doughy blue eyes that resembled the color of sugar cookie frosting. I didn't have children of my own but always enjoyed spending time with them when I had the chance.

"Shhhh," I said. "There, there."

I joined a couple other baby-holding passengers on a small processional loop from the bathrooms in the back of the plane to those in the center. As I walked, I rocked the infant gently and spoke to other baby-walkers. One of them was a stewardess who introduced herself as Olya.

From what I gathered, Olya was the infant expert among the day's flight crew. She held not one, but two babies in her arms and still managed to make small talk with me. She was impressed with my ability to put the babies back to sleep and didn't believe me when I told her I had no children of my own.

When I'd put the first baby to sleep, Olya barked at another flight attendant to assign me to a second one. We embarked on another lap and I asked why there were so many crying babies on that particular flight.

"That's a two-part question," Olya answered dryly. "The high number of babies here is because of the rise in adoptions coming from your country."

It turned out the children were immigrants heading to the United States to be with their new parents.

"The second part about why they are crying," Olya began. "This is because they are from poor communities in Russia. Their families could not always afford to give them milk when they were growing up so these babies are used to drinking tea and they haven't had any for a while."

When I asked why Olya and the other flight attendants didn't simply serve the babies tea from the airplane's kitchen area. She laughed at me and said, "Because our tea is not strong enough as they are used to."

I didn't know how valid what Olya told me was but it didn't matter. How much of her attitude could be attributed to her Russian heritage, her years on the job, or just catching her on a good day, I couldn't be sure either. All I knew was that I enjoyed how she made the best out of a potential nightmare situation.

When people travel, the focus is almost always on the big picture: the sights, the food, even a special event. Rarely do travelers revel in the little in-between moments, even those that are potential incredibly uncomfortable, as opportunities for connection. I patted and bounced the second infant until sleep finally came. I thanked Olya for the conversation and she thanked me for helping the plane get back to a state of quiet.

Soon we would all arrive in New York. We would be corralled into different groups based on where we came from. We would wait in lines. We would collect our luggage and we would go our separate ways. The spell would be broken and we'd return to our daily lives.

When I had finally returned to my crammed seat, wedged myself into position, and started to consider my entertainment options, the sound of a baby crying was music to my ears. It was only a couple minutes before the flight attendant came to my aisle. She didn't have to say anything. She just handed me another soft bundle.

The child, the stewardess, and myself all shared a certain look: one of mutual appreciation. It was nice to need and be needed. Even if you're on an uncomfortable flight from Moscow to New York, the sharpness and authenticity of travel connections can make you feel like you're in a dream you never want to wake up from.

A Suite in Sydney

"When Tina Turner visits, she stays in the same bed," I told my father who stood in the doorway of my suite at the Hyatt Regency in Downtown Sydney.

He grunted and nodded his head the way he had when my mother told him something he marginally enjoyed was being prepared for family dinner.

I cleared my throat, "At least that's what they told me downstairs."

The two of us were on our first ever trip abroad. I had been traveling extensively for more than decade but most of my miles had been spent on my own. This was one of the first trips I'd ever planned and taken with someone I already knew. But the way he appeared in the doorway, staring not exactly at the bed I motioned to but past it, made me feel as if I was meeting him for the very first time.

"You okay dad?" I asked.

He didn't shake out of his trance until I walked up and put my hand on his shoulder. The trip had been planned to give my dad a bit of respite from my mother, who had been sick for some time. He'd remained by her side constantly and wore the exhaustion on his face. Though my mother's condition was worsening in the hospital back home, we were assured she was stable enough for my father to take a much-needed vacation with his son.

"Yeah," he said, unconvincingly. He placed his hand on mine as it rested on his shoulder.

Our trip down under began in New Zealand. We flew into Auckland, rented a car and saw the town. The trip was different. Normally I'm incognito. I travel alone. That's how I roll. Although I often travel alone, I never feel that way because I'm my own best friend. That's my gift. Being with my dad was a change. Sometimes I felt confined. As we drove around town there were things I wanted to do but knew they wouldn't interest my father. Early on in the trip I even began to worry if I could handle the journey ahead. Traveling with someone felt so unfamiliar. Thankfully, we left the city before long and headed to visit the country's famous thermal mineral wells.

We had arrived at our hotel in Rotorua late. The director of sales and marketing had met us in the front. I was a young professional in the tourism industry and my status didn't hold as much weight as I wished it did. When my dad jumped into our conversation, it irked me at first but I soon saw the wisdom in his tactics. He's tall, with a deep voice, broad shoulders, and olive skin, just like me. My dad has a good personality. He's funny. I'd like to think I get my personality from him but he outshined me often on the trip, as he did that evening in Rotorua.

Before I knew what happened my dad had charmed our way into our own private suites with mineral whirlpools in the back. The sales and marketing director was smitten with him. When we left, she was blushing.

The next few days were exactly the relaxing getaway the doctor prescribed. We spent hours in the hot springs, mud pools, and watched the area's many geysers erupt. It was serene but the relaxation didn't last long.

I'd heard Fiordland National Park was one of the most beautiful places on the planet. At over 12,000 square kilometers, it's also the largest national park in the country and, aside from Death Valley in California, bigger than all the national parks in the continental United States (Alaska has a handful that are larger). The only way to cover the vast area featuring majestic fiords, a friend had advised me, was by airplane.

We arrived at the small airfield to find our plane waiting for us. The Cessna was open and had a Japanese couple sitting inside ready for take-off. I took the seat at the tail end of the plane and my father jumped into the copilot chair.

We made small talk with our fellow passengers about our holiday experience the day before. We spent Christmas in Queenstown, the closest hub to Fiordland National Park and a gorgeous place in its own right. Not unlike Swiss mountain towns, Queenstown sits at the convergence of several snow-capped mountain ranges and although it was summer time in the southern hemisphere, it was still a fitting setting for a Christmas dinner. After we enjoyed turkey and all the regular fixings, we took a tram to the top of a mountain where there was a church.

"The priest asked me to do a reading," my father spun around from his copilot seat told the eager couple. "And I did such a good job they even asked my son to read!"

"I think they just thought our American accents were entertaining," I joked back.

The husband nodded their heads politely and the wife snickered nervously. It was obvious they hadn't understood the story but my dad didn't break stride.

"Hopefully the pilot will ask me to help him with the flying," he said, grabbing the controls.

This time the couple didn't laugh. Thankfully, the pilot arrived then to wash away the awkwardness. He gave us our safety discussion and we were on our way.

As we began to take flight, I felt so happy to be traveling with my father. My preference for solo travel had precluded me from so much enjoyment with him. I told myself we ought to have taken a trip like this sooner.

We flew through Dusky Sound first. The fiord was serene in the early morning, the water below seemed calm. The pilot told us about the wales, seals, dolphins, and penguins that frequented the area. All of us passengers gazed out the window, hoping to catch a glimpse of the wildlife.

Before we arrived at the famous Milford Sound — which Jungle Book author Rudyard Kipling called the eighth wonder of the world — we arrived at the area's largest fiord, curiously called Doubtful Sound.

A thick fog hung over the water and we struggled to see the scenery clearly. The pilot brought the plane low into the fiord so we could get a better view. Beneath the clouds we saw steep, green cliffs jutting into the water. The view was vaguely sinister. I understood why the word "Doubtful" was included in the name.

The pilot made sure we all got our fill of the view and began to climb back upwards. As we climbed, the plane slowed down. The engine began to struggle to find power. The whole plane began to shake.

"Buckle up," the pilot ordered.

The plane surged again and the couple began to panic.

Rumbling in my back seat, I saw my dad scramble to examine the controls. If something happened to the pilot, he would have to fly the plane.

"We may go down," the pilot shouted, his eyes staring at the mountain straight ahead of us.

My jaw tightened. The couple screamed again. I held my breath as the plane's engine coughed again.

The airplane paused for a moment. I braced myself, expecting it to fall. Right as I exhaled, the engine roared to life and we began to quickly pierce through the fog. Soon we safely passed over the mountain.

Our visit to Milford Sound went off without a hitch. The weather cleared. The stunning beauty of the nature reserve almost made us all forget the frightening experience. In fact, I hadn't even thought about what happened until that moment when my father stood in the doorway of my suite in Sydney.

There, I witnessed the weight of the plane experience finally hit him. Maybe the whole weight of the trip hit him then. Maybe it was the weight of his whole life. He looked at me with watery eyes and said nothing. Then, he embraced me.

"You're okay," I said, tightening my grip on my father's back. "You're okay."

The two of us stood there for a long time. Later we'd see the Sydney Opera House. We'd go to Tasmania and see all the people dressed like the 60s and 70s never stopped. We'd have a layover on the way home Hawaii and go our separate ways for a few days. But for that moment in that suite, I felt closer to my dad than I ever had before.

Even for those people in our lives with whom were already close, a trip can deepen and widen a connection. When you have a near death experience with someone on a trip like that, the connection can become profound. When that someone is your father and your mother is slowly dying a few thousand miles away, there aren't words to adequately describe the clarity that profound connection brings about life and what to do with it.

A Gulet in Marmaris

"Aren't you worried?" I asked the shirtless Danish gentleman with his arm swung over my shoulder.

"About what?" he responded, before tipping his champagne flute into his mouth.

"About the lack of wind," I said. "This doesn't really seem like a great day for sailing."

The Danish man, who I met no more than ten minutes earlier, took his arm off my shoulder and adjusted the sunglasses on his face. It was a beautiful September day on Turkey's Mediterranean coast. The month was one of my favorite for travel because most folks on summer holiday have returned to their homes to start another year of work or school. A place as stunningly beautiful as Marmaris would have been loaded with tourists a few weeks earlier but as we stood on the wooden deck of the man's Gulet boat, all that stretched out before us was lush hills and open seas.

The man waved me over to the controls of the gorgeous wooden vessel. He pointed out that the eighty-foot boat was rigged with a diesel-powered engine. He explained that the two giant masts were more for appearance than functionality. He never actually used the ships sails. We didn't need wind for this excursion.

I joined my friends on a comfortable rounded couch toward the back of the ship. I'd met up with James and Sally in Istanbul but three of us had known each other for years. We'd always talked about taking a trip together and when Sally's Danish friend invited us to Marmaris we felt it was time to put words to action.

In Istanbul, we visited the Hagia Sophia, Grand Bazaar, and reached a consensus that the Alexander Kebab — a dish of thinly cut lamb that was grilled, smothered in tomato sauce and melted sheep butter, then served with pita and yogurt — was easily the best of the kebab family of dishes. After visiting a traditional Turkish bathhouse, we headed off to the airport to fly to Izmir. There, we met a man who drove us the final three hours to Marmaris.

The stretch of coast where the port city sits is often called The Turkish Riviera. Yet for anyone who has been there or even seen photos of the stunning, translucent waters can understand why some refer to it as The Turquoise Coast. As we rode along, the wealthy Dane told me about the many legends associated with the region.

He started with the story of the Chimera, a mythical fire-breathing monster which looked like a blend between a lion, goat and a snake. Apparently, this creature's birthplace was along the coast line where we sailed but cautioned that if we see the Chimera we should be careful because it's an omen for disaster. Then, he unexpectedly told me St. Nicholas — who later became the basis for Santa Claus — was also born in the region. By the time he got to his third story, I didn't know what to expect.

"You know Mark Antony," he started, as I tried not to be distracted by Sally rolling her eyes behind him. "He gave the Turquoise Coast to his beloved Egyptian bride Cleopatra for their wedding gift, such was the extent of its beauty."

Whether it was true or another fable, it at least made logical sense. Despite my many travels, I struggled to find an equal for the gorgeous expanse of turquoise water and lush hillside surrounding us as we sat on intricately upholstered cushions. The more the day wore on, the more I felt I was in my own mythological tale.

When you're in your hometown or even your home country, there is a track you're comfortable and familiar with staying on. For the most part, you go to the same kinds of neighborhoods, eat the same kinds of meals, and hang out with the same kinds of people. Travel allows you to test other waters without any real consequences. This flexibility allows you to make connections with people at the far reaches of your realities, whether in terms of personal interest, profession, or socioeconomic status.

I looked over at my friend James. He was as used to traveling luxuriously as anyone I knew. We'd met years ago in London. He came from wealthy Pakistani stock and he traveled with a different budget than most people I was used to sharing the road with. $10,000 for a couple weeks away from home for him was the equivalent of me treating myself to a nice steak. It was nothing.

Beside James sat Sally, helping herself to the cheese and fruit spread that had been prepared for our afternoon on the Mediterranean. The two of us had known each other for long enough for me to know most of her life story. She came from a humble Midwest American upbringing. In college, she met an engineer who she later married. The two of them moved to Cairo for her husband's job in the oil business and over the years climbed the ranks of the company to become one of its leading — and best paid — executives. Unfortunately, the newfound wealth pushed Sally and her husband apart and they eventually divorced, though she still lived in Cairo to be close to her kids.

James occasionally smiled as the Gulet hummed along the water but it wasn't long before he pulled out his cell phone and started tinkering around. I'd long noticed how Sally carried a certain disdain for the luxury she'd become accustomed to. She began to sort through the cheeses and fruits she deemed undesirable, tossing more than she probably needed to into a nearby wastebasket. Sometimes, like on that day on the Gulet in a place as gorgeous as Marmaris, you got the feeling she would trade it all in to be on a hammock under a big oak tree somewhere in the middle of the United States.

Since I hadn't known our Danish captain and his other friends long enough to know much of their story, I was left to my imagination. Maybe they had done this kind of thing their whole life, like James. Maybe they were newer to the world of wealth, like Sally. Most likely their story was an entirely different one, with its own ups and downs, that led to that very moment hosting us — all of us so very far from where we began.

Once my sheer astonishment of our luxury cruise had subsided, I found comfort in our connected presence there on the Gulet. In all likelihood, it wouldn't be the last time most of them traveled in this style but it was entirely possible that it could be mine. Perhaps the husband in one of the couple's I'd just met felt the same because he began to drink so much champagne that the Dane started to hide the good bottles from him.

I came to discover from talking to the man's wife that sailing made her husband nervous. When he was nervous he drank. The two had flown from Istanbul as we had but only after a short layover from their initial flight out of Copenhagen. It seemed the drastic change in climate was something they'd gotten used to after many summers in a row traveling to Marmaris to join their friends.

James and Sally joined in the conversation, everyone a little friendlier now that the day had worn on and the champagne had made its mark. The woman's husband eventually became so drunk he began falling over. Every time he fell, he would blame the host for playing a trick on him. The host would profess his innocence and then the whole scene would begin again.

Soon the whole of the boat was watching the show. Observing this Danish man argue with another Dane on the Turkish coast with a Pakistani-born Londoner, an American who called Cairo home, and a smattering of other folks who could have easily been from anywhere on the planet made me feel right at home. It didn't matter how vastly different our day-to-day realities were. In that moment, we felt as though we were on the same page in the same book.

I'm just glad we didn't share what came next.

The drunk man finally reached his limit and hurled himself against the back of the ship, letting out the little lunch he had over the railing, sullying the pristine waters of the Mediterranean.

"To answer your first question, I think it was probably good it wasn't windy," The Dane grinned as he changed his course to head back to land. "Then we would have probably had to turn back much sooner."

"True," I said. "Maybe Chimera is also nearby."

A Hut in the Amazon

"C'mon Ed," my Israeli travel companion said. "I'm just asking what you think of the guy."

I kept my mouth shut and churned my heavy legs through the dense jungle.

"Hey," his fellow countryman added. "We told you how we feel about him, we just want to know how you feel."

It was my second full day in the Amazon jungle. The sun hung high overhead but it might as well have been just grazing the tops of the trees of the jungle canopy above us. The guide led our small group consisting of two Israeli men — who'd just finished their required military service — and myself through a section of jungle on the bank of the river. We were taking the long way to our accommodation for the evening, which was set to be with a local tribe.

The day before the three of us had experienced some of the most unreal moments of our traveling lives. We swam with the Amazonian river dolphins, which are either gray or pink depending on their age and gender. The older males are generally a brighter shade of pink and we saw plenty of them playfully swimming in a calm river tributary. Dolphins are beautiful creatures wherever you see them, but seeing a pink dolphin was surreal. The water we swam in was refreshing in way I hadn't expected but as soon as we got out, we had to reapply bug spray and sunscreen. Simply existing in the Amazon was constant work, it was a wonder so many tribes had survived there for so long.

During a lunch of freshly caught river fish, we were visited by a pair squirrel monkeys. The fuzzy beasts looked like aliens determined to steal the papaya slices that came with our flakey fried fish. They would latch onto the table or our limbs like leeches. The only way to pry them off was to dangle a banana provided by our guide in their faces.

All in all, the whole day had been incredible. Of course, I'd also developed a friendly report with my travel companions as we experienced all the Amazon's wonders together. By the time we laid our heads down beneath our mosquito nets in a small lodge at a dock town after the first day, I was sure the three of us were going to get along swimmingly throughout the remainder of our week-long tour. That's why I had vied for extra time when deciding how I was going to answer a question about then-U.S. President George W. Bush.

"Well," I said, when they'd prodded me a third time in the day about it. "I just don't think it really matters what I think or don't think."

I wasn't about to get dragged into a conversation about politics in a country far away from either of the ones we came from. Not only that, but there were so many different plant, bird, and insect species zipping by at any instant, I considered every moment there precious. There was no room for a political discussion.

"What do you mean?" one demanded.

"I mean you two are from Israel, a country thousands of miles and an ocean or two away," I continued. "I'm a long way from home too and here we are together in a third country, Brazil, smack dab in the Amazon jungle. Who cares about George W. Bush?"

It might have been my imagination but I swear I remember the guide even snickering at that point in the conversation. Either way, the Israeli's had shut their mouths.

Sometimes I think the interconnectedness of the world today has been both the best and worst thing that's happened to us. It's the best because my very being in the Amazon depends on the ease of travel and porousness of certain borders that a globalized world has brought on. At the same time, the connectedness caused an unnecessary riff between my travel companions and I when we should have been basking in the moment — heavy and sweaty as it might be.

When we finally came to the village, none of us realized we'd arrived. Exactly six straw huts laid before us in a clearing. The small town we had stayed in the night before now looked like a booming metropolis compared to this micro-settlement. The city I had arrived in, Manaus, seemed like a universe away. It had been called the Paris of the Amazon when many wealthy Europeans brought their families with them to chase the rubber trade. They also brought their culture and arts. That's part of the reason Manaus itself is a booming city of over two million inhabitants instead of a backwater port town for Amazon tourism. Yet most tourists, myself included, visit the city only as a stopover to travel upriver toward the smaller settlements that have survived for thousands of years beside the world's largest river.

Now that I was in the native village, I couldn't believe it's tininess. We were directed to place our packs in one of the identical wooden huts. It was raised about four feet of the ground by a pair of stilts to compensate for when the river flooded. After we placed our things down, I took the opportunity to separate myself from my travel mates to take a break from the tension building between us.

I took a walk, staying close to the village as I'd been advised. A few small wooden boats sat tethered together in a small bay nearby. There were two hastily constructed soccer goal frames about thirty feet apart from each other in one of the flatter, clearer areas. I saw two children peeking out at me from behind some bushes near one building that had some smoke drifting above it.

The sun was going down by the time I climbed the stairs to the house that turned out to belong to the village chief. When I walked through the door, the guide welcomed me to sit down as the children scurried and hid behind their mother in the kitchen. She worked a giant wok of manioc flour the Brazilians called *farofa* and used as an accompaniment to most dishes.

Our guide told me about how the women do most of the work in these indigenous Amazon communities. Her husband, the chief, lounged around and exchanged small talk with the guide and his kids. None of them seemed to have a care in the world despite the guide telling me how during the rainy season the alligator-like giant reptiles called caiman sometimes swim into their homes.

What did these people know of George Bush? What did they care what happened in American politics? It seemed to me they had plenty to deal with right there in their own village without having to worry about the world's problems. Why would they bother with anything more than what they had to deal with?

Our simple dinner of farofa, fish, and local vegetables was served on a banana leaf platter on a nearby section of the floor. The Israeli's joined us after their short rest. We made small talk about the meal and no one brought up the conversation from earlier. The children laughed at us while we ate and we made funny faces at them. Soon enough they were bored of their foreign guests and ran outside to play in an Amazon night that would have scared me to pieces as a child.

The Israeli's announced they would be retiring early. The guide and I wished them goodnight. I stayed without more good cause than a desire to bask in this small arrangement for just a little longer. The wife began to clean up after our meal, bringing some of the small plates to the wash basin at the other end of their small hut.

Out of habit, I picked up the dish I ate from and brought it to her too. As I did so, the chief and the guide laughed at me. I stopped in my tracks as the wife took the plate from my hands.

For a moment, I felt a tinge of offense. Here was this capable man lying on the floor while his wife did all the work. But then I looked at myself, sweaty and dirty and covered head to toe in insect repellant. Somewhere I still carried the weight of the political conversation from earlier.

I laughed at myself too.

Sometimes connections we make abroad, just like those we make at home, don't turn out the way we want them to. Sometimes we only have a few minutes or hours of good report with someone before things change. There was nothing to be upset about.

On my way out, instead of grabbing the Israeli's plates and taking them to the washbasin, I left them on the floor.

A Waiting Room in Berlin

"I'm sorry sir," the secretary told me. "It's late, we only have two doctors working now. You must wait a bit longer."

I let my frustration out through my nose, in a long, controlled exhale. I mustered the best smile I could and took my hands off the cold hospital counter. I returned to my seat and put my head in my hands.

No one enjoys spending their time abroad stuck in a hospital waiting room. Not just because they would rather be out doing more exciting things, but also because needing medical attention in a foreign country is no fun. People can say what they will about the American healthcare system but, for me, there is no where I'd rather be when I need to see a doctor. Unfortunately, we don't always get to choose when and where we get sick.

As I rubbed my cool hands against my hot face, I overheard a couple voices. The waiting room was mostly empty but a few chairs away sat an older gentleman and his younger companion. Based on the way he'd angled himself against the thin-padded chair and the way she fussed with his posture, it was clear the man was experiencing some significant back pain. I had a share of kinked necks in my time but that evening my concern was whether something I ate or drank was to blame for the tantrum my stomach was throwing and if anything could be done about it.

Earlier in the night I had visited one of Berlin's many famous nightclubs. The city is a hotspot for Europe's best DJs and there is a club scene that popped up to support it. The sheer spectacle of the nightlife is worth the visit for anyone who is fortunate enough to visit the city. If you can bear a bit of morning grogginess, the clubs are worth staying at until the early morning hours when clothing begins to shred off clubbers as quickly as their inhibitions. Few places offer dancing and people watching opportunities as prime as those at a Berlin club during an early Sunday morning.

My enthusiasm might have gotten the better of me in the form of my preferred Hendrick's Gin. The liquor's unique blend of juniper, rose and cucumber is invigorating. Mixed with a little tonic and lemon, the beverage is a great refractor of a nightclub's neon lights which flash against the clear concoction's ice cubes and bubbles like a delicious disco ball. I'd followed the late-night crowd out into the morning light and capped the evening with a Döner Kebob.

Chunks of spinning rotisserie meat exist in street food the world over. Mexicans refer to theirs as *al pastor*, or shepherd style, and is usually pork with a slice of pineapple on top used for tacos and quesadillas. The Greeks take slices from a slab of rotating lamb and put it in a pita wrap with cucumbers, tomatoes, and tzatziki sauce, calling it a *gyro*. A similar snack in Arabic is called *shawarma* and is popular among Lebanese communities across the globe. Yet most sources claim it all began with the Döner in the Ottoman Empire or modern-day Turkey.

Across Europe, but in Germany in particular, Turkish immigrants beckon late night crowds with their delicious Döner Kebobs. Far from the plated kebobs you can find in Istanbul, the style I enjoyed in Berlin after my night of clubbing was more a quick-served, have-it-your-way assortment of fillings and condiments jammed sideways into a pita. I reveled in the deliciousness of the Döner as the dawn turned into morning before heading back to the Ritz Carleton falling asleep full and happy. Unfortunately, the combination of Hendrick's and Döner was less kind on my stomach. By that evening, I came to understand it wasn't a condition I could simply sleep off.

Instead of replaying the previous night's activities in my head any more times than I already had, I moved a few chairs over to a new seat just one away from the couple in the hopes of distraction as much as any lasting connection.

"Is he okay?" I asked the woman.

"I think so," she said. "But it keeps happening and he can't sleep."

"I can sleep," the man jumped in. "I just can't lay down."

A sliver of silence passed between us then but the moment it was over the three of us all shared a collective chuckle that was loud enough for the medical assistant to jump out of her chair and ask if everything was alright. Once we'd assured her everything — besides our long wait times and our ailments — was under control, the three of us got to know each other.

It turned out the man was Italian, having grown up in Rome. The woman was originally from St. Petersburg, Russia. The two had moved to Berlin separately several years earlier. The city has a magnetism in Europe for the young and the old, the business and the artistic minded. It made sense then that the woman, a graphic designer, and the man, a writer, would meet in Berlin and fall in love.

"Tell me the story of when you first met," I requested after we'd been talking for about half an hour. We were no longer simply passing the time until the doctor could see us. There in the sterile waiting room of a German hospital that betrayed the country's trademark efficiency, we were engaged in a genuine connection.

They looked at each other with the same unapologetic fondness some of my fellow club members had eyed their Döner's the night before. Then, they told me their story. Mere blocks from the hospital at *Kunstbibliothek Berlin*, or the Berlin Art Library, the couple met pursuing their various passions. The writer had been diving into some old Italian periodicals the library had collected. The graphic designer had been exploring into the library's collection of images from the early days of photography when *pictorialism* was popular.

"I was flipping through a magazine," said the writer, motioning as he spoke in a stereotypically Italian way. "And it was like she popped out of the page of the best story I'd ever read."

"He says it in a more magical way," the Russian girl said, matter-of-factly. "He really was looking at some old book with a pair of tweezers and I approached him more out of curiosity than attraction."

"The pages were crumbling already," the man protested. "I didn't want to make it worse with my paws."

She laughed as he cupped her dainty hands with his massive ones. The movement shot some pain through his spine and he immediately writhed. She stood up and began to gently rub his back. Almost on cue, I felt a sharp poke in my stomach. The three of us were so locked in our conversation we'd forgotten our bodily ailments but they hadn't forgotten us.

A couple hours had already passed but the medical assistant gave no indication that our wait was ending any time soon. The man's back pain settled down again. I decided it was my job to keep the conversation going for all our sakes.

"What's *pictorialism*?" I asked.

"That's a good question and there is no single answer," she answered, as she continued to rub his back. "There were many people in the art world who criticized photography for only being a recording of reality rather than an interpretation of it that left room for artistic expression."

As she spoke, I noticed my stomach pains subside. I concentrated on her words and tried to understand the concepts. Design, to her, was art. It was a reinterpretation of reality but it had grown so functional and practical for many businesses that she felt the art in it was vanishing. She had frequented the collection of pictorialist images at *Kunstbibliothek* to encourage her to believe that design could return to the place where it is recognized as art, just as photography had.

Our discussion seemed to reinvigorate the man too. He asked if I wanted to read some of his writings, which he had translated to English himself — since the two had to communicate in English, both spoke it quite well. I told him I did and we exchanged information right there in the flimsy hospital chairs.

When I read his writings later, long after we had both been seen by the doctor and I had left Berlin, they enthralled me. He wrote about travel. He wrote about love. He wrote about life. They'd been widely published but it wasn't until he sent me an unpublished poem a few months later that I truly appreciated his craft.

The poem was called, "The Man with The Stomach Ache," and was as funny and graceful and surprising as our long conversation had been. It was also about that meeting. The character was based on me.

The connections we make when we travel can be so powerful. They can help us pass through tough times. They can inspire us to pursue our dreams. Even if they develop in a hospital waiting room in a foreign country, they can offer a lasting impact and a lifelong friend.

Part II: Adventure

In the late 1960s, just as commercial air travel became mainstream, airline companies funded a researcher named Stanley Plog to figure out why people traveled to the places they did. He interviewed, surveyed and tested 1,600 subjects. In 1974, Plog published an article called "Why Destination Areas Rise and Fall in Popularity." In it, he used his study's data to break travelers into three main categories: allocentric, mid-centric, and psychocentric.

Though these were loose categories, they became the standard for Tourism & Hospitality industry thinkers. Psychocentric travelers tend to restrict their travel to places they already know, plan things more rigidly, and avoid risks. Mid-centric travelers aren't afraid to try new things or leave the schedule a little loose, but are, by no means, adventurers. It is the allocentric travelers — the ones who shun planning and organization — who rarely like to go to the same place or do the same things twice. The allocentrics are adventurous.

Looking back, from my very first experience in adventure travel at eleven years old, I was clearly the allocentric type. Now, on the surface, taking a train across the country wouldn't rank highly on the adventure meter for most adult tourists. Yet, as a young boy growing up in Texas — who only went as far as Albuquerque on family road trips — traveling by train to the East Coast one summer was an exciting journey of epic proportions. It whetted my appetite for adventure travel that I've spent my entire adult life trying to satisfy.

It was decided one summer that the younger of my two elder brothers, my maternal grandparents, and I would take the train to Philadelphia to see my cousins. We arrived at my grandparent's farmhouse in Albuquerque and spent one night. The next morning, after a light breakfast, my grandfather gave me the job of calling the cab company.

By this time, I had become more known for my secretarial skills. I was great with organization and arranging details. I called and requested a cab. After a few minutes of preparation, we were out on the road, waiting. Time dragged on. My grandmother checked her watch. My grandfather, who was pacing back and forth with his hands behind his back, turned and asked me to call another cab company. I did what I was told, we waited again, and no cab came.

This whole scene repeated itself a half-dozen more times before a cab finally arrived. Funnily enough, just as the first one came and we began to load our bags, another pulled up, and then a few more. Soon, there was a small fleet of cabs in front of my grandparent's farmhouse. It was during the ensuring spat between my grandfather and the angry drivers, which ended only as we needed to speed away toward the train station, that I realized the limits of planning when it came to travel adventure.

On the platform, I made small talk with a young, pig-tailed girl who wore pink ribbons in her hair. She was traveling to Kansas City with her mother and our family's first stop would be to transfer in Chicago. We began to make faces at each other to lighten the mood as we boarded the huge, steel dragon of a vessel. My brother and I were wearing blue jeans and tank tops, but I felt like we might as well have been dressed in a knight's armor as we set foot on the train for the first time, such was the sense of the fantasy we'd found ourselves in.

From the first moment the train began to sway and rumble, I fell in love with locomotive travel. The rocking was a new experience for me, not unlike the comforting sensation I had as a baby in the arms of his parents, except there was excitement all around us. We had a sleeper compartment but the whole train was our playground. Where our family's Buick station wagon was a confined space — where cries of "he touched me," "he keeps hitting me," "Mom!" were the norm — in the train I felt free. I could move around all the time. I could go to the entertainment car, mess around with people in the dining car, and otherwise run about without purpose. It was more like the freedom I felt in the roadside hotel than in our car on the road trips.

The porters were funnier than hell. They wore shiny uniforms with the names of the train line — ALBEQUERQUE-CHICAGO — stitched to their clothing. They loved their jobs and they were good at them. They would cuss at us and run after us because we would wake everyone up at three or four in the morning by poking our fingers, hands and heads through the compartment curtains, waking our poor fellow passengers up at all hours.

Aside from the family going to Chicago, there was also an older man traveling alone. He was writing in his journal always — during meals, late at night, whenever I saw him. I wondered what he was writing about. We never spoke. I felt what he was doing was somehow sacred. He was the only one spared from our hijinks.

When I grew tired of running around — or the train's security guards had accosted us and sent us back to our compartment — I enjoyed staring out the window at the vast country passing by before us. The rocks and cliffs of the desert eventually began to flatten out as night came. By the morning, the cactus had turned to corn fields and I was told we had entered the Midwest.

While my brother, exhausted from our exploits, and my grandfather slept, my grandmother and I went to go get breakfast in the dining car. It was all fine china and white tablecloths, even for the morning meal service. There were pancakes, bacon, and omelets but, as I was wont to do, I ordered the most expensive thing on the menu. When the eggs benedict arrived, I sunk my fork into the over medium eggs and tasted the first tangy bite. I was stunned. It was incredible. The way the softness of the English muffin, the salty slab of pork, and lemony hollandaise sauce meshed together was a total culinary awakening.

"You never know what you'll find," my grandmother told me, watching the delighted expressions on my face with every bite. "When you're on an adventure."

I swept up the last of the yolk and listened to my grandmother as she told me the story of the only cruise she went on in her life. Boats were another mode of transportation I had dreamed of for as long as I could remember. During my nightly baths, I scooted around a little plastic boat in the water, and pretended I was sailing to all the destinations on my beloved globe. I listened intently to my grandmother's story of riding the cruise ship from Los Angeles to Hawaii.

Once they'd arrived, she said, they had a celebratory luau. They danced hula, enjoyed traditional Hawaiian ukulele music in the flickering light of tiki torches, and ate a feast. Everyone loved the kalua pork and the tropical fruits like pineapple and mango but there was one item everyone agreed was ghastly.

"It was called poi," she explained. "It had a kind purple-grey color and it was made from a root named taro, which was like a yam or potato."

She told me how all her fellow cruise passengers made awful faces — the opposite of the ones I was making as I bit into my eggs benedict — while they ate it. Their reactions made her both frightened but also intrigued. She grabbed a big spoon full and quickly shoved it in her mouth.

"I had to try it," my grandmother said. "Because it was part of the adventure."

She didn't love poi at first, but she said by the end of her time in Hawaii, she found herself craving the pasty substance. Her story echoed in my mind as we made our way back to our compartment. I made it a point from then, to this very day, to always try something new when traveling, to make the experience an adventure.

When we transferred trains, I was struck first by how massive Chicago's Union Station was. Its colossal scale dwarfed the quaint platforms we'd stepped off at the Albuquerque station. I looked up at the massive skylight and was almost run over by the throngs of passengers as they walked purposefully toward their destinations. It was my first moments in a major city. My grandparents led us swiftly to the platform where we would board our train bound for Philadelphia, then told us we could explore if we stayed close by.

I walked around in an astonished daze, running my hands along the gorgeous wooden benches and the massive walls of the place. I couldn't believe someone had built something so grandiose and gorgeous. It was like a cathedral to my new love of train travel. My mind raced wondering what Philadelphia station would be like, or for that matter, New York's famed Central Station.

Meanwhile, my brother had befriended a pack of kids and they were playing tag, weaving all around the station. As it got closer and closer to the time until our departure, I decided I should tell him it was time to go. The problem was, in all his competitiveness — he wanted to teach the big city kids how good Texans were at tag — he ignored our schedule. I pleaded with him to come but he brushed me off. The minute hand on the big clock kept ticking and I finally began to whine.

"If we don't go now," I screamed. "They'll leave us."

"No, they won't," he answered, running past. "They wouldn't do that."

"Oh, yes they will!" I shouted back.

This went on for a few more minutes before I was finally able to convince him to leave. My prediction was right, the train had begun to churn forward on the tracks just as we arrived, stepping with our cross grandparents onto our car just as it was getting up to speed.

Even after I'd calmed down after our near-miss, I still felt my heart nearly beating out of my chest. Although I was no more thrilled with my brother's behavior than my grandparents, I had to admit the whole experience of jumping on a moving train was exhilarating. That something as scary as being left behind in a major city station was possible, the world felt more real and exciting. The moment showed me that even close calls could make a trip even more adventurous.

Philadelphia, once we arrived, felt much smaller than Chicago. The train station was no less beautiful. The ceilings were massive with matching tall pillars that held the place up over the stunning marble floors. As we exited, I watched the different destinations flip by on the boards and listened to the announcements for the trains headed to Boston, Washington D.C., and New York. There was a huge, sprawling fountain outside 30th street station. All these locals were hanging out by the water, trying to cool off in the mist on the hot summer day in the city.

It was my first time back east. I was just a boy from a small town in Texas. My uncles and cousins picked us up at the station and we rode with them to their home in Dover, Delaware. I watched out the window as the huge city flew by, telling myself one day I would be on those trains to Boston, Washington D.C., and New York.

In Delaware, we went to the beach. We went bowling. We saw our cousins and played with them. We went to restaurants and even an amusement park. Then, we went home.

We took the train back the same direction but the trip was horrible. The vacation was over. I was let down. I was going back to reality. We could enjoy the same things on the train on the way home but it wasn't the same. The excitement had disappeared. It was over.

I realized then why adventure is such a big part of travel. The destination is okay but I like the journey along the way more than the destination. You can like the different characteristics of the destination, for entertainment, culture, friends, family, a business conference, even the way it can provide spiritual guidance — but there is something special about the journey.

To be sure, not all travel is adventurous, whether we are allocentric, midcentric, or psychocentric, or if we disregard the categories all together. When we move about for business, we rarely get to have those experiences where we can laugh in the face of danger, or do something we never thought possible. Yet, even the little moments where we can try a new food or jump onto a moving train, can give us that shot of adrenaline that makes the journey, not the destination, so important for adventure.

Perplexed Outside Beijing

I'm sitting beside a sleeping woman on a rumbly bus dashing through the cloud of bronzed air that surrounds Beijing. The woman has her camera slung over her neck. Though it's morning, there are sizeable sweat stains under her armpits, which I only notice when the bus slams to a stop and then surges forward again, sending her body flying backward and forward like a noodle made by a roadside street hawker. Reckless motorcyclists wail around us like mosquitos to a slab of exposed flesh but no matter how loud or long our driver honks or how intensely he swerves, the woman doesn't wake up.

She's exhausted. The day before she'd wondered around Tiananmen Square, examined Mao Zedong's tomb, and explored the Forbidden City. At night, she watched a Beijing Opera and ate the world's most famous duck not named Donald: Beijing Duck (or *Beijing Kao Ya* as they call it). I know all of this because I was there with her too. Forget green tea, there isn't enough instant Nescafe powder in all of China to keep an American alert after a day like that.

The only thing preventing me from joining my couple dozen foreigner companions in catching a few winks before we arrive at our next destination is my excitement. When I booked this two-day group tour covering all the major sites in Beijing it was for three reasons:

It was cheap.

It was efficient.

I would get to finally visit the Great Wall.

Tour groups, especially ones so full of older or more inexperienced travelers, aren't my preferred travel style. As someone who has spent a lifetime traveling, I prefer to be on my own so I can dictate the pace and the vibe of my experience. Tour groups don't usually make sense for me, but in this case, I was leaving Beijing in two days and had been won over by a friend who had booked the condensed-itinerary tour the year earlier.

The driver slings our bus around a curve and the sleeping woman suddenly begins using my shoulder as a pillow. I didn't know this woman. Our interactions up to this point have been an exchange of pleasantries (she was a school teacher from the Midwest) and exactly one request to snap a photograph of her standing in front of Mao Zedong's giant portrait. I can't speak for everyone, but for me, this is enough of a report to allow a little shoulder snoozing. While she sleeps, I glance out the window at the thinning urban landscape, as it gives way to brush.

Despite having visited China many times over the years, somehow, I had not found my way to the world's longest structure. In addition to tour groups, many frequent travelers despise major tourist attractions. This isn't just because they've often already seen the attractions on some other journey in the past. It's because tourist attractions can be a time-consuming and headache-inducing experience. It can also be a shoulder-wetting experience as I discover there in my bus seat.

I feel something soak through my shirt and tilt my head to the side to see a steady stream of drool emitting from the mouth of the sleeping woman. I quickly nudge her back toward the middle of her seat. A quasi-stranger leaning their head on your shoulder in their sleep is one thing, human fluid is quite another. I consider myself a nice guy, but I'm not, "Go-ahead-and-drool-on-me," nice — infants exempt.

The small wet spot didn't douse the fires of my excitement. Although I am well-traveled, I'm not the type of traveler who avoids tourist destinations as a hard and fast rule. There is a reason these places are so popular — they carry a cultural and historical significance. They symbolize something. As much as crowds and price gouging can undermine their appearance, it is impossible to ignore their importance.

At heart, I'm a travel romantic. I'm in it for the adventure. If sitting on a crowded tour bus with a woman drooling on you doesn't sound like an adventure to you, dear reader, then we are on the same page. Still, the journey and the destination both come into play when adventure is on the agenda.

What location packs a bigger historical punch for adventurous panache than the Great Wall of China?

When the bus parks, I must caution myself against the instinct to crawl over the drowsy tourist bus passengers and scurry up to the wall. I follow the protocol, wait through the briefings, and take the chairlift to the structure.

Once my feet are finally against the stone of the ancient barrier, the travel romantic takes hold. Like a kid pretending his playground is a castle, I bent down and peer through the loopholes scattered every few dozen feet along the walkway, imagining what those who patrolled the wall saw on the horizon when they glanced through. Some sections of the wall were built as the 5th century before Christ. Others were restored or rebuilt during the Ming Dynasty around 1500 AD. I feel the weight of these eras beneath me. It charges me up. I see another watchtower in the distance and I decide what must be done. I'm a runner, after all.

I start to jog, waving at the confused Chinese tourists as they turn their cameras way from the wall and toward the tall American running past them. Elsewhere in China, this attention had sometimes been overwhelming but this time, I enjoy it. I'm running along the Great Wall.

Once I exhaust myself and our time at the wall is up, I join the others, including the sleeping woman — who complains to another tour bus passenger about how tired she still is — at the luge slide back toward the direction of the parking lot. As I wait in line, I take one last look at the wall snaking its way over the mountains. Despite all the hype and all the crowds, I am enamored by the scale and charm of the mighty stone dragon.

After our group retreats to the buses, we are whisked to a small restaurant nearby. As is the case for many tour groups, the meals are included. The ordering process is streamlined where there is a set menu already in place and each table receives the same dishes. Eating in China can be its own adventure. The sheer amount of different kinds of dishes, various cooking techniques, seasonal ingredients, and specificities of the many regional cuisines is mind boggling. The evidence is in the smells alone, which cascade from the kitchen as we sit down. The sleepy woman yawns and takes the seat immediately across from mine.

Plates slide in front of us — scallion topped egg with diced tomato, braised green beans, charred spare ribs, and sour bamboo shoots. These dishes are arranged on a lazy Susan at the center of the table, ready for spinning and sharing. I am substantially hungry after my wall adventure. Just, as I pick up my chopsticks and prepared to dig in, a loud squawk rings out through the restaurant. I spin my head, expecting to see a bird at the window.

No bird on the sill, just a cook taking a smoking break with his attention turned toward our table where two waiters stand. One holds a boiling pot of water and the other wields a very unhappy bird by its two thin legs. It wiggles around too much to be sure but it vaguely resembled a blackbird. The first waiter sets the pot down at the center of our table. The second — against a collective gasp of our tour group — lowers the bird, which lets out one last squawk before being released into the pot.

In the fraction of a second before the bird splashes into the boiling water, a few things happen. First, I feel my eyebrows raise along with many of my campions in sheer awe of the audacity to bring a live bird to a table of foreigners who, no doubt, find it at least slightly disturbing. Next, those without raised eyebrows, manipulated their facial features into reactions of comprehensive disgust. Then, finally, amongst the squawks overheard at other tables, the sleeping woman from the bus faints.

When the smoke clears and everyone has posited their various theories about how best to take care of our fainted group member, we begin to pick sparingly at the food. Some select a few green beans. Others grab a tomato here and there. The white rice seems to suddenly become everyone's favorite food.

Everyone, that is, except for me — I'm famished.

I dive into the pork. I ran along the great wall. I pile the eggs and tomatoes onto my plate. I need nourishment. I shovel other items I can't distinguish into my mouth.

Then, as nearly everyone else sets their eating utensils down, I stare at the untouched mystery bird soup at the center of the table.

Feeling eyes fixate on me, I pick up the spoon and lower it into the yellow broth. When I lift the steaming liquid back up, I gaze at the empty space where the sleeping woman had fainted. Her chair is unoccupied, as she has returned to the bus early to rest before the drive back to Beijing.

I pause and smile, thinking about how happy I am to have come with this inexperienced tour group to this tourist trap. Then, I slurp the soup into my mouth.

It tastes strongly of adventure.

Captivated Above Cuzco

"I'm not saying they had to be aliens," I overheard a young man telling his traveling buddy as a small group of us hurried up a stone path. "But have you seen how tall the indigenous people are here?"

I rubbed my eyes, trying to banish the last bits of sleepiness from them as we moved in the dark toward Machu Picchu, the ancient Incan citadel in southern Peru.

"I'm just saying it's an explanation that makes sense," the young man said, his friend seemingly too tired to muster a response.

I had camped near the same pair of travelers the short night before. They, like me, had just visited the mysterious Nazca Lines prior to setting off on their hike to Machu Picchu. Created sometime between 500 BCE and 500 AD, these lines are called geoglyphs and were made by moving reddish pebbles on the ground to expose the lighter colored earth underneath. More than one hundred shapes were crafted by the Nazca culture and some depict animals, flowers, insects, and human beings.

These geoglyphs are gigantic in size when seen as a group, measuring 450 square kilometers in total, but with the largest ones over 350 meters long, even individually the Nazca Lines are a marvel to behold. Many people visit the Nazca Lines by airplane to get the best view of their magnificent shapes and detail, which was what both my early morning hiking companions and I had chosen to do.

"What about the scientist who recreated the lines using tools available at the time," the other young man finally blurted out as our small group joined another, all of us heading the same direction — up. "Doesn't that rule out the alien involvement?"

"Not necessarily," his friend said, noticeably giddy to finally be engaged in the conversation. "It doesn't explain how they've survived all this time."

"It's a desert, there's hardly any wind there, didn't the pilot say it was one of the driest places on Earth?"

"Okay, fine, but even if you can answer all the practical questions, riddle me this: why did they make these huge things in the first place?"

His friend fell silent again. It was a question scientists and scholars had been trying to answer for decades. There were ritualistic, astrological, and religious explanations but none seemed to be fully accepted in the scientific community nor in the community of travelers. The idea that they were made by or for aliens, a preposterous hypothesis when taken on its own, becomes less so when considered from the information available.

Walking along an ancient path like the one to Machu Picchu, having a conversation about aliens and ancient history, rushing toward the top of a mountain to catch a sunrise — these are ingredients for great adventure. It's not impossible to find them in your own backyard, but it's certainly easier if you're willing to move around a bit. Adventures like these are the reason so many millions of people spend so much money, time, and resources on travel.

As the sweat began to form on my brow, creating a contrast to the crispness of the morning, I smiled about the aliens and about adventure. Did it really matter who made the lines and why? No. Some say money is the lubricant of life but I'd say it's curiosity. What's just around the corner? How does it feel to be in a place like this? Why was Maccu Picchu abandoned? I'm as curious as they come, which is why I set out on adventures like these to satisfy my inquisitive cravings.

"Uh oh," the friend finally said. "We've got company."

Our burgeoning group suddenly encountered another — and this time much larger — collective of hikers. We were now less of a group and more of a mass, falling into a tight, fast line like a stream of ants toward a pile of abandoned picnic snacks. I could tell it was going to get dicey.

When it comes to adventure, people can get a bit greedy. After spending so much money, sometimes saving for years to take the trip of a lifetime, it comes as no surprise. You only live once and if you've already traveled thousands of miles to do or see something, you are naturally going to want to make it worth your while. After all, any trip to any adventurous locale might be the only one you ever make. You want to make the best of it, right?

The pre-dawn hours, when everyone is still groggy from having just woken up or delusional from having stayed awake all night, aren't the best time for jostling. Yet, there we were, a few dozen of us, pushing and shoving along the path toward *Intipunku* — or The Sun's Gate. Myself included.

When it comes to adventure, I'm no different from any one else. I had heard the sunrise in Machu Picchu was one of the best in the world. Being that I already traveled to Peru, schlepped my gear on the few day trek into the mountains, and woken up at the appropriate time, there was no way my adventure wasn't going to include a sunrise over the ancient ruins.

Part of my insistence comes down to intention. I'd come to Peru for adventure. There are times when I'll visit a big city with the hopes of making connections, but when I'd arrived in Lima earlier, that was the last thing on mind. The Peruvian capital is the third largest city in the Americas, after Mexico City and São Paulo, and had the shanty towns stretching out from the airport to prove its status as a megalopolis. Oddly enough, I did find a small adventure in the city itself, and not one I was expecting.

Before they moved en-masse to Brazil, Japanese immigrants were welcomed in Peru to make up for a lack of labor. With the economy in Japan difficult in the period around the turn of the 20th century, these immigrants came to Peru. Generations later, the Japanese Peruvians have left their mark on the country, with one eventually becoming President. However, where I experienced a bit of their cultural heritage was at a restaurant in Lima's San Isidiro district.

As a huge fan of ceviche, I leapt at a dish called Tiradito. Sliced as thin as they would be for sashimi or carpaccio, fish was served in a spicy sauce between two staples of ancient Peruvian people: a sprinkle of quinoa and a bed of potatoes. I was admittedly bewildered by the restaurant's Japanese-descended staff running around speaking Spanish to each other, all in the setting of a South American megacity. Yet, the moment I put in combination in my mouth, I understood the multicultural culinary adventure that's elevated Peruvian cuisine above most others in the region.

In this way, adventure, like connection can be planned or serendipitous.

If you're travel plan makes room for adventure, it will come. Embrace it and you'll receive something satisfying and — occasionally — delicious.

As I remembered this incredible meal in Lima, my adventure on the Andean steppes continued. The sweat had now encompassed the whole of my shirt, as the air began to hint at the warmth that brings the start of the day. Additionally, our marching-line-of-ants, started to behave more like one. People had stopped asking permission to pass one another and were simply overtaking them. The procession had taken the mood of a race.

I wasn't immune to the pushing and shoving either. Adventure can be like a drug and I needed my fix. I just hopped I didn't hurt anyone.

We finally arrived at Intipunku, the place where so many famous photos of Machu Picchu are taken. Few of the photos I'd seen ever captured how incredibly crowded it was, crawling with tourists in every direction, snapping their photos in the thin morning light.

There seemed to be only one specific area where the sunrise could be properly witnessed and we all gathered there, in a crowded bunch. Thankfully my height meant I wasn't going to need to worry about where I stood in the crowd, just that I remained there. I noticed the two travel buddies who had camped and hiked near me stood right in front of me.

The one pushing the alien theory took off his daypack. His shirt was soaked through with sweat as well. A crudely drawn alien was drawn on it with a message underneath. It wasn't until the sun rose, the crowd cheered, and the pictures had all been taken that I finally got a chance to read the text.

"If it's an adventure you want," it read, the alien pointing its finger toward me in the spirit of an extra-terrestrial Uncle Sam. "Then it's an adventure you shall have."

Wealthy in Buenos Aires

"It makes me sick," a retired-aged woman announced in perfect English.

Standing there, impeccably dressed, in the ornately furnished living room of her former high-rise apartment, she continued, "This place is worth two or three grand a month and you're getting it for $300."

I didn't know how to respond. I tried to crack a smile but that didn't help. She slid her wavy blonde hair out of her face, her piercing green eyes a shade lighter than the green dress she wore. Her gaze rendered me mute.

"I'm Rosa by the way," she said, extending her hand. "And I might not sound like it, and I am happy at least someone will be living here — even if it's not me."

Around the turn of the century, the value of the United States Dollar tripled in Argentina. On the one hand, things were suddenly a third less expensive for Americans visiting the country, as I had chosen to do. On the other, Argentine's like Rosa who managed real estate properties, felt the impact tenfold as rent values plummeted.

When I found the listing, I had no idea I would be moving into the nicest apartment she managed — the very one she had been living in for more than two decades — and I almost wanted to scrap the whole arrangement because of how she looked at me. Yet, after we conversed for a while longer, it became evident that she was merely lamenting the downturn of the economy and she was truly grateful to have any money coming in. It was a strange position for me to be in and I felt, on more than one occasion since I had arrived in Buenos Aires, that I was playing the part of the rich man without any prior rehearsal.

Travel allows you to be whoever you want to be. It can also enable you to have adventures you could never afford at home. When people complain about the cost of travel, I'm always quick to remind them that it can also be a real money saver, depending on what kind of adventure you seek.

It was like a movie. This woman stood in front of me with wavy blonde hair, in an immaculate emerald dress, shaking her head as she signed her apartment over to me for a period of three months. The total cost was less than one thousand U.S. dollars. The same sort of place in the same sort of neighborhood in a European or American city might have cost me around twenty times that amount — and I might have enjoyed it less.

The proceeding few weeks felt as if someone had cast me to play the lead in a film about a guy who suddenly discovered he was rich beyond his wildest dreams. The apartment was situated in the Recoleta district of the city. The neighborhood's European architecture and colonial history were the primary reason the city became known as the Paris of South America. From the famous cultural center to the basilica with its cinematic cemetery beside it, I would walk the streets near my new digs and feel like I was in a decorative dreamland.

I quickly took to the Buenos Aires lifestyle. I started to visit the parks, reading and studying how locals served their preferred caffeinated beverage yerba mate, using a combination of loose leaves, a gourd (made of ceramic, wood, and calabash), and a filtered metal straw. I soon had a gourd of my own and shared my maté whenever the chance arose. Between breakfast and dinner, I enjoyed the savory empanada pillows and choripán, small sandwiches filled with chorizo smothered in zesty chimichurri.

At night, I dined out at the nicest restaurants in the nicest neighborhood in town. Argentina is legendary for its steaks and I ordered the fattest, juiciest cuts of meat on the menu. Not an evening meal would pass where I didn't sample some of the country's famous Malbec, feeling free to toy around with a restaurants higher priced options. When the bills came, with totals as few as $6 and only as much as $20, it was difficult not to feel as if someone wasn't hiding at a nearby table with a camera waiting to reveal the whole affair had been a practical joke.

But it wasn't. This adventure of newfound wealth was merely a lesson in why watching currency rates matters for flexible travelers. There was nothing about Argentina that was particularly calling out my name. I hadn't fallen in love with a Tango instructor or needed to visit a faraway family member. I had merely wanted to know what it felt like to live like a king for a few months and in Buenos Aires I found out.

"Careful though," a man named Gus told me one night. "In a country like this you can be wealthy one day and withered the next."

Gus had been raised in Philly. He headed south years earlier as a way of escaping something from his past he could never quite put into words. I gathered that it might have been legal trouble — and he wouldn't be the first to escape to South America from impending legal proceedings, just ask the Nazis — but never wanted to press him on the subject. Gus wasn't the type of guy to want to talk about himself in explicit terms.

We became fast friends because of our mutual love for beef (Texas is famous for steaks and the proof for Gus's hometown is right there in the name: Philly Cheesesteak) and shared a fair amount of lunches and dinners together. It wasn't until a month or so of knowing the guy that came to learn Gus, like Rosa, had invested heavily in real estate in the city. The night he'd warned me about the flimsiness of my newfound wealth, we'd shared a couple bottles of Malbec, and soon he was alluding to his own precarious investment position through wine stained teeth.

"Sounds like you've got a nice set up," Gus told me of my apartment. "But let me know if you want a change of scenery or are looking to buy. I've got places all over the city and now is a good time for you, I reckon."

That was the first night I covered for Gus's share of the wine bill but it wouldn't be the last. Our dinners became darker. His stress was visible. Not just in his face but in the sheer amount of wine he'd consume in a single sitting.

"When the peso devalued this time," he said one particularly dark evening. "There was no coming back. Not for this country, not for me."

About a week later, after failing to get a hold of him by phone I walked along the widest avenue in the world — Avenida 9 de Julio — toward Gus's apartment. I'd only ever visited him once at his fantastic penthouse but I figured I could find him there, sleeping off a hangover and see if I could cheer him up with a guard of yerba maté or a choripán.

"Gus esta aqui?" I asked when the maid answered the door to his place.

"No," the maid said, stepping back, perplexed. "No, lo siento."

The woman paused for a moment and looked me over. I wondered if she was trying to size me up the way Rosa had. I scratched my arm nervously, not knowing how to proceed. Then, before I could ask why she was sorry she blurted out, "El Señor murío."

"He got married?" I said in English. He hadn't told me about an impending wedding. From all I knew, he might have been running from a spouse in the States when he came down here in the first place. Then I asked her who he married, "Con quien?"

She stared at me curiously, like there was something wrong with me and there was. It wasn't until she went into the kitchen and got the newspaper that I realized my Spanish hadn't come as far as I thought. *False Friends* are the term linguists use to describe two words in different languages that sound or look the same but have a very different meaning. I had made a similar false friend error earlier in my time in Buenos Aires when I overheard a woman say she was *embarazada* and I figured she was just embarrassed. It turned out that's the word for pregnant.

Murió, which I wrongly assumed meant getting married, was the past tense of *muerto*. I looked at the paper, which talked about a man who had a heart attack on the subway. It turned out my friend Gus was dead.

I thanked the maid, apologized, and left after what had to have been one of the strangest interactions of my life. Wealthy or no there is nothing like death to bring you crashing back to reality. I stepped out of his building and back onto Avenida 9 de Julio.

Crossing the street that day felt like crossing the sea. Much of the remainder of my time in Buenos Aires felt similar. Whenever I rode the rickety old metro I thought of Gus. I thought of how he had accumulated and then lost a fortune. I thought of how even though he escaped whatever he was running from, there was no escaping death.

Eventually my adventure as a wealthy man was over and I readied to return to America. In the end, the experience reminded me of that which is priceless: life itself. Wealth comes and goes. We can't take money with us when we die, no matter how much or how little of it we have.

As I flew away from the city, I looked down and hoped the best for Rosa and her realizations.

Lost on Fraser Island

At first, we thought they were tiny lights. A few bobbed around in the bushes a good distance from where we were having our fire. I noticed, as they came closer, that the lights came in pairs. Two by two they multiplied, until there were so many I couldn't count them all and neither could my six traveling companions who were reacting with various levels of fear.

The group of four girlfriends from Malaysia and Singapore huddled together and screamed.

"Oh, just ignore them," the only other American in group, a younger guy from North Carolina added. "They're not going do anything."

I wasn't so sure.

"Remember what the lad said in our briefing," the tall, red headed — and bearded — Irishman said, standing up. "If you see a dingo, you stand up, cross your arms, look right at them and you don't move."

The Carolinian stayed put right where he was, behind the group of frightened girls, pretending to poke at the fire but gazing out toward the shiny lights. The Irishman didn't add the second part of what the tour guide had mentioned in the tour briefing before the seven of us set off in our SUV for a week on Australia's famed Fraser Island. I stood up all the same.

Amidst the many warnings about all the things on the Australian island that could kill us, including the heat, getting lost, and eating the wrong plants, he spent considerable time tackling the issue of wild mammals roaming the island. In addition to swamp wallabies, bandicoots, and flying foxes, dingoes, Australia's famed wild dogs, inhabit the island in larger numbers compared to other places in the country. Dingo attacks on humans first made headlines in 1980 when a two-month old baby was killed in the Northern Territory. A few attacks on Fraser Island occurred later, including the death of a 9-year-old boy. In short, contrary to how our nonchalant Carolinian travel companion was reacting, there was some cause for concern, as we'd been told.

"You don't show fear in your eyes," the guide had said, concluding his dingo troubleshooting speech. "Because if you show fear they will charge you."

We were all scared, myself included. When I took my place beside the Irishman, I did my best not to show it. At this point, there were too many sets of eyes to count. Once our vision adjusted to the darkness after we'd been staring at the campfire telling stories for so long, I saw the outlines of the beast's golden fur as they roamed the perimeter of our campsite.

I crossed my arms as they drew closer, then I tried my hardest to look at the whites in their eyes. I pretended they were regular dogs who had just misbehaved. This helped lessen the impact of their nasty growls and snarls.

A week-long camping adventure on the world's largest sand island sounded great when the plan had been presented to me. Yet there have been moments on many trips I've taken where I got a bit more adventure than I'd thought I could handle. Watching the speed with which the dingoes began to dart around us at made that one of those instances. Try as we might, the Irishman and I couldn't stare such a big group of dingoes down at once. Eventually we were bound to lose sight of one or two.

In a flash of fur nearly the same color as the flames of our fire, a trio of dingoes sped across the open area beside us and snatched a few items from a bag of food negligently left exposed.

"Holy hell," the Carolinian cried, the animals brushing his leg as they ran past.

By the time we turned around, saw the thievery, and turned back, the dingoes had all vanished.

"Weren't ya supposed to take care of that bag?" the Irishman asked me.

"Not me," I said. "I was in charge of the cooler."

Our eyes all turned to the Carolinian who shrugged his shoulders. The tour guide had also repeated to us the age-old lesson wherever in the world one might choose to camp: the best way to avoid attracting any unwanted wildlife is to keep your food stored safely. After the group had settled down back down, I was just happy we'd gotten away unharmed but the girls still chose to sleep in the SUV rather than their tents for the night.

Few places conjure adventure like Australia. I should have known better than to expect the night with the dingoes to be the biggest fright of our trip to Fraser Island. The next day, our last full one of the trip, the group was taken to the most remote part of the island for a day of exploring.

There are those who say that any trip away from home can be an adventure. Others might have a higher threshold for it and plan carefully for a trip outside their home state or even abroad. For me, adventure in the truest sense of the word doesn't begin until you are off the map.

As we all set off in our separate directions for the day of exploring, I chose a direction deliberately away from the others. I am, by nature, a lone wolf. I needed to roam at my own pace if I was to enjoy the last of my Fraser Island adventure to the fullest.

Perhaps the Carolinian could smell the risky adventurer in me. Maybe he really did, as he was quick to explain, just happen to arrive at the same set of sand dunes as I had to eat the sack lunch I packed with me a few hours after everyone parted ways. I was not sure. What I was sure of is that once he asked me if I could spare some water we were in for a long, uncomfortable afternoon together. It was also clear the sun wasn't about to let up on us.

"Sure is hot," he told me as he jovially sipped from my back-up canteen. "Didn't realize this whole island trip was going to be a grueling as this — was picturing something a bit more hammock related."

He thanked me for the water and I put it back in my pack.

There was still time to do a little more roaming before I needed to head back to the meet up point. As I expected, the Carolinian asked if he could tag along until we returned. It would have been cruel of me to turn him down because I knew he would have only responded by admitting his being lost. This decision was one of those seemingly gracious ones you live to regret.

It became evident as the two of us started to trek together that his function as a companion was to behave as a fountain with a steady stream of complaints spewing out at all times. Some of his gripes were social: *Weren't the women in our group terribly annoying and loud? Wasn't the big Irish guy a bit too full of himself?* Others were biological: *Didn't my feet hurt too? Blisters? How sunburned did I think I was getting?*

I wish I could say I was a reliable compass regardless of my emotional state, but that's simply not the case. The more he complained, the more irritated and distracted I become. It wasn't long before I had completely lost track of where we were. It was a fact that I wouldn't be able to keep from him for long.

"We haven't seen anyone else in helluva long time," he said. "And didn't we just pass by this same section of shoreline?"

There it was. I had dreaded admitting I was as lost as he was but there was no way out now.

"I'm don't think so," I cleared my throat. "But regardless, I think we may be a little lost."

The truth was had no idea whether I'd seen that strip of sand or any others at that point. I was sunburned. My feet did hurt. To many matters worse, our water supply was quite low, mostly because the gratuitous-sized sips he took from the canteen.

I was already beginning to plot my escape from him, expecting his response to my admission of being lost to be more complaining. I wasn't about to risk my life out there with that guy. If it came down to it, I was going to suggest we part ways. Yet he hadn't responded at all. I just heard him trotting along behind me silently, the sun nearing the end of its run for the day.

Then, I heard a sound I hadn't expected. I didn't turn around until I was sure. When I finally did, there he was, failing to quiet his budding sniffles and shutters. The obnoxious Carolinian was crying. He was terrified. He just wanted to get home safely.

A wave of responsibility suddenly hit me, not just as the older of the two of us but as the person who knew how to keep their cool. Even though I'd almost lost it only moments earlier, it was time to keep it together. If we were both going to adventure another day, I needed to come through.

Once the sun had completely dipped out of sight, the relief from the heat was quickly doused by the realization that neither of us packed lights. We would have nothing to light up the sparkly dingo eyes.

We also had more pressing concerns. Both of us were incredibly thirsty, out of food, and completely exhausted. We hadn't expected to be out this long. The exploration was supposed to last approximately eight hours and we were close to hour number twelve.

I was worried. I was frightened. But we kept on. I told myself that keeping it together mentally when you're lost on an island isn't a lot different than forcing yourself to stand with your arms folded in front of an animal that might want to attack you. I searched for the whitest grains of sand, like I had the spaces in the dingo eyes, and kept marching on.

Before we hit hour thirteen, we came upon a house with a light on. Inside we called our group, told them where we were. They blamed me for our getting lost and I didn't bother trying to tell them the whole story. I needed to save my energy for other adventures.

Wild Near Nairobi

It was five o'clock in the afternoon. The sun sagged in the bright blue sky. All the animals at Ambolesi National Park headed toward the watering holes to drink. I was in my tent, getting ready for my first dinner when I felt a booming sensation. Then, I heard it.

I stuck my head out from my tent. No more than thirty yards away a fully-grown adult elephant stomped to a stop at a small pond. Before his trunk broke the surface of the water, my vision began to blur.

I was on my first safari. Aside from seeing them in zoos and on nature shows, I had never witnessed these almost mythological animals with my own eyes in the wild. Elephants can be dangerous. They can charge and crush you if they are frightened. Yet this one was just as calm as the evening breeze that blew by and a sight so beautiful I'll never forget it as long as I live. By the time the elephant finished drinking and headed back the way he came, tears had been streaming down my cheeks for a good five minutes.

Adventure can be more than fun, it can be profound. Sometimes the thrill of seeing or experiencing something incredible is secondary to a new understanding you receive about the world itself. For me, it was difficult to have a safari adventure a massive increase in my appreciation of nature.

Seeing a majestic creature like that, up close, was the first step in a journey that shifted my perspective about animals in general. At the time, I was living at the Hotel Norfolk in Nairobi. My weekdays were spent teaching tourism at a hotel school in the city. Most of the students would graduate and find work in the safari park lodges that hundreds of thousands of international tourists visit annually.

After my encounter with the elephant, I made it a priority nearly every weekend to go on safari at one of the nearby wildlife parks. My second trip included a visit to the Maasai tribe. Known for their semi-nomadic lifestyle, members of their ethnic group inhabit the region on both sides of the Serengeti along the border with Tanzania and on the Kenyan side, the area is known as Maasai Mara National Reserve. The region is home to the largest terrestrial mammal migration on earth and, as such, when I was invited by a local chief to join them for a meal one afternoon, I expected meat.

I sat down in this hut, made from vertical wooden sticks and a straw roof, and I presented to them a goat I had purchased on their behalf. It was a gesture I was recommended to make by a local in the city. Then, I received a bowl full of a granulated white powder in water. With my first sip, I could tell the meal was going to be more about making sure I saved face than salvaging any kind of enjoyment. I smiled as best as I could at the other Maasai in the hut — including one who held a traditional spear I feared he might hurl at me if I dishonored the chief by not finishing — and lapped up the foul-tasting mixture as quickly as possible. When we were done, the chief thanked me again for the goat and presented me with a carved wooden walking stick as a token of his appreciation.

After lunch, I joined a guy from Botswana who wanted to take a walking safari. He had been working in Kenya for years at the time. When I voiced my concerns about not having the protection of a vehicle he brushed off my fears and said I'd be fine.

"Don't worry," he assured me smiling. "You're with an African!"

"I'm from Texas," I responded. "I won't be fine until you put a 22 in my hand."

"Your new walking stick should suffice," he laughed.

I shook my head and off we went. The afternoon was crisp and bright. I stayed close to him in case a lion emerged out of the vast Serengeti. Before long, we arrived at a Rhino game reserve. He brought us over to one rhino which was laying down on all fours.

"Pet him," the Botswanan told me.

"No thank you," I said. "Petting a rhino is something I will not do."

He insisted there was nothing to worry about. The man pet him to show me everything was fine. I was still suspicious but he kept pushing me. Finally, I decided that if I was going to make the most out of this adventure, I better pet the damn rhino but I was going to do it as safely as possible. I worked my way around the rhino until reached toward it's backside, far away from his horn and mouth. The instant I reached out to touch its leathery skin, it got up off the ground. I nearly shit my pants.

Later, as the Botswanan laughed all the way out of the park at how scared I got, I learned one valuable lesson. If a rhino ever does lower its horn to charge you, all you have to do is laterally step out of the way because they can only charge things straight in front of them. They can't zig zag. In the end, when the rhino stood up all it did was grunt and lie back down.

Back in the city, I was invited to another meal. This time, a group of local expats brought me to a restaurant called Carnivore. Upon entering the place, it's hard to miss the enormous open fire pit in the middle. Cooks managed various animals on spears that were made to resemble the ones I'd seen with the Maasai out in the bush. I took a seat and the processional began.

Not unlike a Brazilian *churrascaria*, waiters hustled about offering all-you-can-eat meat options, slicing off meat slabs in whatever amounts you request. The meats on offer included more conventional options like cow, chicken, pork, and goat. I tried some of these and enjoyed the comfortable tastes I had grown accustomed to my whole life. Then, the man next to me motioned toward a skewer heading our way.

"Zebra," he announced.

It was the first time I'd had a moment of hesitation in my entire meat-eating life. Though I respected the sympathies of vegans and vegetarians I'd met in my life, I had never seriously considered whether-or-not to eat cooked meat when it was placed in front of me. On another safari, I had ridden across the Serengeti on horseback. As we rode along, a zebra came up beside me and matched the steps of my horse. For a few minutes, I felt a strong connection between myself, my horse, and the zebra beside us.

Like my moments with the rhino and the elephant, that moment had suddenly changed my relationship with animals, and as one zebra approached me in charred form, I was a bit lost on what to do. My hosts gave me no time to decide.

"Here ya are," said one man, taking a slab of the freshly cut zebra meat and slapping it on my plate, the blood still gushing from the tender center. My decision was made for me.

Like my experience in the tent, I didn't want to lose face. I ripped into the piece of meat and chomped it down with my molars. I did the same with samples of crocodile, wildebeest, and hippo. By the time I finished the latter, one of my dinner mates leaned forward, and informed me that the hippopotamus is the number one killer of humans in Africa.

"That's it fella," he said. "Eat 'em before they eat you!"

Toward the end of my stay in Nairobi, I decided to visit Aberdare National Park to the northwest of the city. After so many rugged adventures, I felt it was time to treat myself to a bit of luxury so I opted to stay in a lodge called The Ark.

It hovered above the ground. Wildlife would visit in abundance. Giraffes came to graze. Wildebeest roamed by the thousands. Monkeys hung around at night and were clever enough to grab your passport if you weren't careful. Beyond the threat of losing important documents to a baboon though, I felt more at ease than I had been on my other safaris. I felt like a real veteran but I still had mixed feelings about the relationship between man and beast.

During my first night there, I heard noises again but this time in the far distance. *Womp womp womp.* The sound continued past midnight.

The next morning, I asked someone on the staff at the Ark about the noise.

"Those are the hippos," he said, noticing the fear stretch across my face. "Don't worry though, they stay close to the water so you've got nothing to fear."

No less than fifteen minutes after our conversation, I was up on the deck watching as a group of my fellow guests roamed out by bank. There was one woman who was drifting dangerously close to the water. As if it were a scene from some Wildest Videos show, a hippo suddenly appeared out of nowhere.

Hippos are big and fat, but it happened fast. It got her and started slashing her around. She screamed. Amidst the blood, I caught a glimpse of her leg. It looked a lot like the slabs of meat from Carnivore.

When they freed her, they rushed her to a hospital in Nairobi. I later heard she survived but they had to amputate her leg. The whole episode gave me some clarity on my relationship with animals after all. When it comes to traveling adventure, it seemed, sometimes we eat the animals and sometimes they eat us.

Risky Around Mumbai

Unless you travel back in time to 1920s New York, with the gangs running the streets or 1930s Shanghai, when the French Concession played by their own rules, the image of jazz doesn't conjure much adventure. The music's risqué roots have been watered down today to the point where the genre sits just a notch above elevator music in the minds of most concert goers. That was part of the reason why, as I sat a few chairs away from a quintet of Indian jazz men on my first trip to what was then called Bombay, I was lulled by their swaying rhythms into a false sense of boredom for the first time on my initial trip to India.

Since the wheels of my flight from Zurich touched down and I disembarked into a thick Indian summer alongside around two dozen Swiss nationals, I hadn't felt bored for a second. We'd toured the majestic Taj Mahal in Agra, scarfed up colonial confections in Calcutta, and seen elephants march through the streets of Delhi. This is not to mention that, being the only non-Swiss in the group, I also felt like I was on two trips at once: one to India and one to Switzerland.

Perhaps the moments when these two trips intersected in the most entertaining way was every time we came across a cow in the middle of traffic. The Swiss being so familiar with leveraging cows as a resource for the famous dairy products and the Indians seeing them as sacred set up for some hilarious and confounding confrontations between people in my tour group and the locals. The reverence with which the locals treated the *"smelly-milk-bags,"* as one member of our group was fond of saying, wasn't finally resolved until we'd noticed a Rolls Royce screech to a stop on the way to dinner in Mumbai. Caste system or no, if even the rich and rushing citizens of the county gave the cow the right of way, then it was something the Swiss had to respect.

I'm sure the pizzas on the menu for dinner that evening at the jazz-themed restaurant by the beach also helped. Adventure or no, everyone gets antsy for a taste of home when the images of the cuisine of their cultural heritage are dangled in front of them. I joined my Swiss travel mates, diving deep into a thin-crust pepperoni pizza, taking my own break from the spicy curries and dal we'd been eating almost every meal since arriving in the country.

"This is the best pizza I've ever had," Lucile turned and told me. "And I'm not just saying that. It really is."

Lucile and her mother, Anne, who sat on the other side of her were the two members of the group I'd gotten to know best. The daughter and I, only a few years apart in age, had seemed to have an understanding about the way the world worked and it was nice to have someone with a similar outlook to chat with as we experienced such a complex place. Yet she and her mother Anne, both had their minds set on another kind of experience entirely.

Earlier on the trip, Anne approached me as I took a walk to the hotel pool to take a dip. She had just finished her swim and she asked if I had a moment. What I didn't expect in that moment was for her to propose the most preposterous thing: could I help her change out of her one-piece bathing suit as it had been a bother to put on?

"Well," I had said, clearing my throat to respond to her plea for help. "Why don't you just ask your daughter to for assistance."

Before she responded, Anne searched my face to see if I was giving anything away. I had a pretty good idea of where this was going based on her tone but didn't want to face the reality that the times I caught her eyeballing me during the trip weren't a coincidence. I rolled the dice and played dumb, hoping she'd drop it. I hadn't counted on her persistence.

"You see Edward," she said, spelling it out. "I'd like her to *watch* you *help* me and then maybe the three of us can help each other."

There was no way to get around it. I had to face her head on. We would be scheduled to spend a lot of time together and I had to snuff the issue out right then and there.

"Sorry Anne," I said, trying to choose my words carefully but firmly. "Those aren't the kinds of things I can help with."

64

For her part, she took it in stride. She smiled and wished me a good swim. Once we split up and I arrived at the pool though, I was in no mood for laps. In fact, I felt like I was being watched so I went back to my room.

From that moment until the jazz band stepped on stage and we finished the last of our pizzas, I'd been on guard. The draggy melody coming out of the quintet, my happily full belly, and the waiter's arrival with my cocktail left me in less an adventure and more of a vacation state of mind. I completely forgot about Anne's creepy request and gazed out the window at the still waters of Back Bay, the Arabian Sea just beyond.

Adventure can get exhausting, especially in the developing world: India's lack of sanitation, the abject poverty, and the relentless heat. While so many things about the country also fascinated me from the cultural and religious traditions to the Moghul architecture, sitting inside this Art Deco, spotless, air-conditioned restaurant with gentle, if somewhat unremarkable, jazz tunes playing made me relax. Some members of the group headed back to the hotel. I stayed and ordered a second cocktail, as did Lucile and Anne.

After about an hour, once most of the guests and the band had gone home, the owners of the restaurant joined us for a few more drinks, as did the remaining patrons from nearby tables. As we all got to know each other in that way only late-night drinks by the sea can provide, I discovered they were fascinating people. The patrons were regular customers and they'd known the owners for years. They had gone on trips together, often aboard a freighter one of the guys owned.

How interesting it must be to have your own freighter, I thought.

The more we talked, the more they seemed to be taking a liking to Lucile, Anne, and myself, the only members of the Swiss tour contingent remaining. They asked about our trip. We told them where we'd been, what we'd seen. Like everyone, they had their own opinions about what we'd done right and what we'd done wrong. We all agreed that a couple weeks in India was not nearly enough to see the country properly.

"It's just too massive," one of the two restaurant owners said, his partner nodding in agreement. "Six months might do the trick."

"Six months?" the man with the freighter said. "I grew up in Mumbai and I feel like I still don't have a full grasp on the place."

That brought the whole group into a big shared laugh. Then, they asked us when we were leaving. I told them we were headed out in only two days.

"It's settled then," said the freighter man. "It's time for you to come aboard the ship and set sail."

I chuckled, then took a swig of the end of my drink as Anne jumped in.

"Can we?" she asked, nearly causing me to choke on my beverage. "Is it nearby?"

Lucile was in and once the restaurant owners pleaded with the group to wait just a minute as they closed-up, it was settled. In what felt like no time — but must have been around four in the morning — we sped over to the ship, went through an intense regiment of security, continued driving the car onto the ship itself, hopped on board, and arrived at the captain's bridge. The man was explaining all the controls, Lucile and Anne were blown away. I was baffled.

"Why don't you guys stay a little longer and come with us," the man with the freighter said. "We're heading out to see at the end of the week. We have rooms you can stay in."

Anne looked at Lucile, in a reversal of normal parenting roles, but the daughter shook her head. She didn't want to encourage her mother's penchant for the outlandish. For the first time since the jazz band swayed me into a traveler's trance earlier in the evening, I remembered our bizarre moment by the pool. It suddenly occurred to me that the three of us had just joined four complete strangers aboard a massive freighter in the middle of the night in a country we were all visiting for the first time.

Thank God nothing happened to us and they soon drove us back to our hotel without incident. On the one hand, you can attribute our good fortune to beginner's luck. On the other, it's obvious we made a risky — if not an outright stupid-decision in accepting a whimsical late-night offer.

Sometimes the adventures we're most grateful for are the ones we manage to avoid.

Devastated at Home

Contrary to content savvy marketing strategies, high-definition images, and screens the size of walls in our homes, adventures almost never begin when we plop down on the couch, throw our feet up, and fire on the television. In fact, there is good reason to believe that television probably stifles the adventurous spirit in us rather than cultivates it. Today the best travel shows can make us feel as though we've been to places we never have and had experiences we never will — so why get up off the couch at all?

Yet one day, when I was 25-years-old, I was sitting at my apartment in Washington D.C., flipping through the television channels, when I stopped on a broadcast that would change my life forever. The Marine Corps Marathon was about to begin. The announcers were interviewing different racers. The runners were stretching their legs. The race was still a way off from starting and I said, out loud, to myself, "I want to do that."

I started running for fun around the time I was finishing up my undergraduate college years. At first, I did it just to stay in shape. I wasn't on a team or in a club. I ran alone. Eventually I bought a decent pair of running shoes. Over time, as I started to up the distances on my runs, I discovered the magic feeling people often call "runner's high." The way, when your body is firing on cylinders, your mind settles into this fully focused pure state of mind — it was something that hooked me good. Not long before I moved to D.C., I told myself I'd found my sport. I was a runner.

While I sat there, watching the television broadcast of the Marine Corps Marathon, and talking to myself, I realized the race start was only a few blocks from where I lived. I can't imagine more than a couple minutes passed between my realizing that fact, throwing on my running gear, and flying out the door. Before I knew it, I was standing at the starting line.

I got in a few stretches and then the gun went off. Suddenly, I was running a marathon. I wasn't officially registered but I ran the course all the same and finished in around four hours.

If I was hooked on running before, that first marathon turned me into a full-blown distance running junkie. I dedicated my early mornings to running. I met friends who I would sometimes run with but even when they weren't around, I would lace up my shoes and pack the miles on the way overeaters pack on the pounds. I began registering for the famous races around the country. I ran the Chicago Marathon, in my record 3:19 time, and I ran the New York City Marathon, in just under three and a half hours.

By the time I got to my 30s, I grew bored with simply running marathons. I joined a race group that also trained for triathlons. I was a decent swimmer and I very comfortable on the bike so I took to the races naturally. For a few years, I signed up for most of the triathlons and half-ironman races throughout Texas and Florida. Between training for a couple of races, I discovered yet another category called *Adventure Races*. These differ from the traditional run, bike, swim format of ironman and triathlon races in that they include things like paddling boats, carrying a backpack, and even camping. I did my first adventure race in Waco, Texas and I had to complete the race with a partner in pairs.

The adventure races were quirky but after a while I realized I was getting less of the "runners high" than I did when I started running. I decided I needed to ditch the bike and the water to get back to my running roots. I wanted to recapture the magic.

For runners, there is the difference between slow and quick muscle twitch groups. The longer the running distance, the more you rely on your slow twitch group. These muscles are more challenging to cultivate, because — as the name suggests — they take more time to build up and train. Almost anyone can fire on their quick twitch muscle fibers and run a hundred-yard dash. They might do it slowly, but they'll do it. Most will be able to run a 5K or even a 10K. Some people can run a marathon but very few people on the planet are able to cultivate and master their slow twitch muscle groups to run ultramarathons.

I began to run ultramarathons. I was drawn in by the sheer scale of a lot of the races. 50 to 100 milers aren't out of the question for many in the ultramarathon world. It wasn't long before I set my sights on the one of a handful of races in America that holds a special place in the minds of the community and generates absolute disbelief outside of it: The Race Across America.

Taking places over 70 days, averaging around 43 miles per day, and covering the full 2100+ miles from the Pacific coast to the Atlantic coast, the race is in a category of its own. It might not have been an adventure race in name but it certainly would be the most ambitious running adventure I'd ever undertaken. I signed up without a second thought. I'd ran fast marathons. I made my mark in the triathlon and ironman world. I'd even completed adventure races. At that point in my distance sport career, I felt there was nothing I could not do.

We started in Southern California. Huntington Beach, one of the iconic beaches of Los Angeles, was the site where the gun went off. The air was electric. Everyone started off quickly from all the adrenaline. The group ran fast through Anaheim and I thought to myself, *we've got the whole country, ahead of us, slowing down might be a good idea,* but I couldn't get my feet to listen to me. The adrenaline and the weight of the moment got the best of me too.

I had a crew with me. We stayed at Motel 6s along the route. I worked with radio sponsors to raise around $50K. We had T-shirts made. There was a website where you could follow my progress. Through the first few days I felt good as I cruised toward Las Vegas.

The night before I was set to arrive in Sin City, I was in the Motel 6 taking care of some budding blisters before bed. Then, some members from my crew came into my room. They wanted to see if we had pooled enough resources to help-out another racer. Maybe I was suffering from heat exhaustion and the physical demands I was putting on my body, but I couldn't see the wisdom in trying to stretch our already thin crew and resources. I'd trained for a full year for the race and every free moment I had from work and training, I spent fundraising. I felt bad for the other racer, but I was worried about the long road ahead.

My crew didn't feel the same way. We had an argument and they left my room. I struggled to sleep that night, trying to get the bad juju out of my head, and focus on the task at hand.

By the time the next day started, something felt off and it wasn't just my sleepiness. Within the first few miles, I started to feel a dreadful scraping sensation — like nails on a chalkboard for your thin, worn layers of skin. The disagreement from the night left me so upset, I completely forgot to fully treat my blisters. I kept on but as the sun grew high in the desert, adding heat to the already difficult situation of my exhaustion and my bloody, raw feet, I feared the worst.

Somehow, there was still down to go. My crew, going completely against what I'd told them the night before, decided to dedicate their assistance to the runner short on supplies. Perhaps they felt I was too cold-hearted in my reaction to helping someone in need. Perhaps they just wanted to spite me. It didn't matter. All that mattered, as the sun continued overhead, was I had more than two full months of running ahead of me and it didn't seem possible.

I did something then that I'd never done in any race up until that point in my life: I threw in the towel. It was too much. About five o'clock rolled around, I could see Las Vegas in the distance, but my feet wouldn't move another inch. My spirit was defeated.

The race director asked if I was sure and I confirmed it: I quit.

I was so upset about my failed adventure I hadn't considered the possibility that my crew would refuse to help me. They continued with the other runner and I was left to find my own way home. It took me three days and two bus tickets before I finally made it. I was devastated. For a time, I wished I would have just stayed parked on the couch all those years ago and watched the Marine Corps Marathon on television.

Triumphant in The Sahara

When I quit the Race Across America, I also decided to quit running. It wasn't only that I was physically exhausted to keep up with my regular routine of morning runs. I was too disappointed in myself to lace up my sneakers. I'm one of those people who holds myself to a high standard. I'd never quit anything in my life and even though the race was a serious — some would say almost *impossible* — undertaking, I didn't know how to process my inability to finish.

For years, the only solution I could come up with was to abandon that part of my life. I went back as if nothing happened. Everything else returned to relative normalcy on the outside. My internal life just wasn't the same when I didn't exercise, but I did my best. I resumed traveling, for work and for pleasure, as I had done before my distancing running career ended.

Things seemed to almost be back to normal when I took a work trip to France. I was simply getting breakfast at a Parisian café one morning, a hot croissant warming my palm, and the flaky crust crumbling onto my jeans with every bite, when I saw a man unfolding a huge newspaper spread at a table nearby. The large desert landscape photographs weren't what caught my eye. Neither were the frames of seemingly endless wavy sand dunes. What caught my eye was a runner in one photo donning a face mask and ski goggles, his scarf slapping against his dirt-stained backpack, as he plunged one foot into the sand and yanked the other one out. The racer looked like a space adventurer who crash landed on mars and was running to stay alive.

The man set down the paper and I immediately rushed over to examine it: "*Marathon des Sables*" read the headline. A familiar feeling came over me, not unlike the sensation that gripped me when I watched the runners preparing for the Marine Corps Marathon on television all those years earlier. I suddenly had the urge to run for the first time in years.

I didn't fly to Morocco immediately and join the race, but I made a mental commitment to take the race on and I had my work cut out ahead of me. The Marathon des Sables — or Marathon of the sands — is almost unanimously considered the toughest foot race on the planet. Over six days, racers complete approximately six marathons back to back, for a total of over 150 miles (250 kilometers). It also takes place entirely in the sands of the Sahara Desert.

Before I could hope to survive such an event — combining my penchants for travel, adventure, and running — I knew I would have to give myself the best chance of finishing. I had to train. I started off by walking long distances. Then I switched to speed walking. Soon, I was back to jogging.

It was only right that I resumed my running career where it ended: in Las Vegas. I registered for the half marathon there and ran it like I hadn't taken a day off in my almost 10 years away from the sport. If it felt great to be running again, it felt twice as good to be racing. I'm a fighter and to be competing again made me feel alive. It was like I had reawakened a dormant monster inside me and it was hungry.

After running that half marathon, I completed two half-ironman races: one in Orlando and one in Corpus Christi. In both events, I experienced difficulties with the water temperatures and logistical struggles with the bike portions, but made up time during the running section to finish far ahead of my projected time. These races allowed me to prove to myself that I was up to the task of running the Marathon des Sables. I registered for the race, the start date was over 11 years since I crashed out of the Race Across America.

In the lead up to the event, I began to do hot yoga, trained in America's most famous desert areas like four corners, and overall felt as alive as I'd ever felt since I began traveling. A good adventure can do so much. Sometimes, it can save your life, or even bring you back from the dead.

The temperature the day before the race topped out at well over 122 degrees Fahrenheit. I double checked that I had the supplies I was going to need while making sure I didn't pack too much. I was told a heavy pack could be the difference between finishing and not. I examined my sleeping bag and tarp — which I'd spread out underneath the tents the organizers would set up after each stage. I had to pack enough food for the full week, averaging close to 3000 calories per day — enough to survive on but too much to weigh me down. I also had to include the requisite distress flare, venom pump (for snakes), and compass.

The next day, I started the craziest and most expensive (around $5000) running adventure of my life. By two o'clock that first afternoon, with the sun beating on me, I began to feel the weight of my choice. I wore one of the white hats you see people use when they go on Safari with a cloth that covers the back of the neck. Over my eyes, I had a pair of trusty Speedo swimming goggles to keep sand out. Then, out of nowhere, a sandstorm hit.

Racers around me began to stop and fix their shoes. They'd prepared them for the threat of sand from the bottom but it was finding its way inside their shoes from the top. It goes without saying that you don't want sand rubbing between your sweaty patches of skin: that combination takes bloody blisters to a whole new level.

Fortunately for me, I'd anticipated such issues when I prepared my race getup. I cut a pair of tights like shorts, covered my shoes with the skinny sections, and duct taped the ends. As I ran, I stayed completely sand free, despite the storm blowing it in every direction.

After we finished the first day, I met my tent mates. One guy, from France and another from England, both had sand issues. I filled them in on my tactic and they thanked me for the help. At the end of each day, there was a medic that came around and checked on everyone. She treated my tent mates' blisters, made sure we were all hydrated, then left as we settled in to sleep.

The next morning, bright and early, it started all over again. On the second day, I witnessed a Japanese woman quit the race. She wept when I passed her. She looked as devastated as I had felt more than a decade earlier when I dropped from the Race Across America. Still, I pressed on.

Later I came across a racer with an entire camera crew. He was from China and I noticed that after each stage he and the crew would smoke cigarettes. I found it a little bizarre, to be running all that distance, and still have the lungs to smoke. It turned out, he was cheating. Through a combination of decoys and a vehicle, the documentary crew was helping this man cheat so they could capture each stage of the race on film without completing the event. It was just like a woman I'd heard about during the New York Marathon who had snuck out of the race and taken the subway to another section of the course, and tried to pretend she finished it. I found out one day when I stopped seeing the strange crew of cigarette smoking racers around that they, like the woman in New York, got caught and had to leave.

The days wore on and despite all the various characters and antics, I kept my focus. By the last day, I felt confident I would finish even as the race continued into the night time. With about two hours left in the race, visibility got bad again. Another sandstorm had swept in and I was exhausted. I felt good enough to keep going, as long as I knew I was going the right way. For a while, I didn't see anyone and the way I had been racing was by following the person in front of me. I was worried I was getting lost. Myself, the Frenchman, and the Englishman had maintained a similar pace so I wasn't surprised when I came across them with about two hours left to go in the race, I was thrilled.

What I hadn't expected was to find them sitting down, shivering in blankets.

"Glad to see you guys out here," I said, catching my breath. "Everything okay, I think I'm lost…"

"Hey Ed," the Englishman said, the Frenchman kept quiet. "We're okay, just taking a break."

A break sounded great. No, it sounded like heaven. Yet I knew if I sat down, there was no way I was getting up. I had to finish right then or I wouldn't finish at all.

"I'm going to move forward," I said. "Is this the right way?"

"We can't tell you that," the Frenchman said. "That would be cheating."

"Cheating?" I shouted. "It's freezing out here. I don't want to get stuck out in the Sahara with no water."

The two men kept their mouths shut and when I realized they weren't going to answer me, we all looked at each other. That one look said more than we ever could hope to say to each other. I didn't waste any more time and decided to press on.

Not long after I caught up to another group of runners. We surged together toward the finish line and when we got there, I cried. I cried out of joy and pain but mostly out of the sense of having coming back from the biggest defeat of my life to achieve my greatest victory.

Thankfully I left when I did. Only one of my tent mates finished after their rest. They both apologized for the mix up after the race and I forgave them. In the end, the Marathon des Sables was more than an adventure. It was more than travel. It was a spiritual experience.

Part III: Spirit

Back in the late 1970's and early 1980's, travel agencies still ruled. Often brick and mortar stores, they were as much a fixture in town as any other business. These places mapped out your journey, arranged your accommodation, and booked your transportation tickets. The better agents could create itineraries no matter someone's schedule, budget, or personal preferences. As time went on, however, they became unnecessary middle men for folks who were willing to handle their travel plans by themselves, especially if it meant saving a little money.

Just as banner ads grab people's attention when they are poking around online for their next vacation now, these agencies put up massive window posters of tropical islands, ancient temples, and any other international spectacle at the worldwide destinations they could send their clients. As I turned from a child to a teenager, these posters increasingly drew me in. I walked by the Texas travel agencies and stopped to window shop, the way fashion lovers fantasize about owning their favorite new releases from a clothing designer. When the agencies were slow, I would spend countless hours inside talking to the tourism professionals, dreaming, and learning about all the places I wanted to visit. For me, these places represented something deeper than a visceral experience. There was something spiritual in the draw that destinations had on me, something bordering the holy.

If connections and adventure are the surface reasons we travel, the deeper meaning for our movement is the spirit. It's internal, whereas the former two are external. For some, that means spirituality — a faith. Muslims travel to Mecca. Christians embark on pilgrimages like Northern Spain's Camino de

Santiago. Chinese devotees visit the eight famous Taoist and Buddhist mountains. Jewish people across the world take their birthright trip to Israel. For the non-traditionally religious, even trips to a national park or a wildlife refuge can be a kind of spiritual journey. The common thread isn't the belief in a certain deity, but a seeking of something beyond oneself.

I began to consider this at a younger age than most. Though my interest in travel had been peeked during my family road trips and train trips across America, it wasn't until my family moved to Brownsville, Texas — a town that shared a border with Mexico — that I began to feel the travelers spirit grow inside me. While my siblings and peers were delving into their various interests — sports, relationships, hobbies — I set my sights abroad. I was so serious about it, that I began to seek employment with far more enthusiasm than most people my age. If I had places to go, I needed to find a way to get there.

Through a teammate of my brothers, I landed a job interview at the local Ramada Inn, which had a restaurant attached. I was only fifteen but I had a clear goal in my head. A couple years down the road, I was going to Europe. There was no doubt in my mind about it.

The manager was the kind of single mother that had at once an iron fist for discipline and a gracefulness to nurture the talent on her staff. Her management style was immediately evident in our interview, where she waved off my lack of experience and zeroed in on my enthusiasm for the work. I was straightforward with her about my savings goals and my traveling aspirations, which she openly appreciated. To her, I imagine, I looked like an ardent believer in the power of the hospitality industry that was willing to do all the dirty work in the name of experience and saving for my big trip.

We had to fudge some dates about my age so I could start as soon as possible, as opposed to waiting until my sixteenth birthday — which might as well have been an eternity to the impatient young man as I was then. From the get go, she was my mentor in earnest, but her son showed me the ropes. He taught me how to set up a table at the restaurant. We discussed the logistics of ringing people up after a meal or a night's stay in the hotel. He also warned me about the unreliable cooks we had in the kitchen.

I faced that challenge early on. One weekend morning, our 24-hour restaurant was slammed. The hotel had been packed the night before and the lobby was a flurry of activity in the morning, most of it consisting of people walking like zombies toward the scent of freshly cooked breakfast and coffee. One of the chefs hadn't shown up, so I was manning the bacon station, then running back to the front of the house to take orders and seat people. At one point, my colleague turned to me.

"I know I warned you about the chefs," he said, throwing me his car keys. "But I didn't tell you that sometimes we have to be the ones to go wake their drunk butts up and get them in here for work."

"I don't have my license yet," I said, but he was already gone.

I wasn't the picture of model behavior, but neither was I someone who actively wanted to break the law. I quickly rationalized the situation with myself. I was already working underage, what harm could a little driving underage cause? It's crazy what people can do when they are true believers in something, and when it came to travel, I was a devotee.

The chef's apartment wasn't far from the restaurant, only a few turns. I walked up to his door and banged on it as loud as I could until I heard a loud groan inside. He came to the door, half dressed, a couple minutes later as if he'd done this a thousand times. He pulled on his shirt as we walked down to the car and we zipped back to the restaurant.

He washed up and got in the kitchen. I resumed my normal position at the front of the house, filling as many drink orders as I could to keep the rumbling stomachs at bay until the food arrived. Even as I ran around serving, I already knew the experience was the type of thing that would put most young people off. What teenager would voluntarily want to go pick up drunk, foul-mouthed colleagues with the free time of their youth? If I hadn't wanted to go to Europe so badly, I'm sure I would have quit on the spot after having to jump through hoops like that.

My boss was pleased with my dedication. She gave me a long leash after I proved myself in the stickier situations. When business was slow, I would read every hospitality magazine I could get my hands on. My boss had subscriptions to all the big ones. I poured over the articles and the photographs about destinations near and far.

"You really want to go into this business," my boss asked me one day, when she found me reading. "Don't you?"

"Yes," I said, emphatically. "I do."

Despite my resolve, I was not immune to the frivolous obsessions of normal American teenage life. I loved clothes. When Polo Ralph Lauren began to make waves, the brand became my weakness. I was drawn to the designs, the colors, and the feel of the company. Even though I'd begun to stack my savings together for my European trip, I couldn't help but dip into the savings one day to splurge on a particularly attractive Polo shirt.

Oddly enough, from the first time I wore the shirt, it felt as heavy as chainmail. It wasn't the material either. I walked around wearing the shirt but felt like I was only fooling myself. For the price of that shirt, I probably could have bought myself another few days — if not a full week — in Europe.

The traveler's spirit inside me knew I needed to repent. At the same time, even though I knew buying more Polo wouldn't suddenly change how I felt, I was still drawn to the new designs as they were released. The clothing shop windows were competing with the tourist agencies for my attention. I knew I had to do something about the perilous situation.

On my day off from the Ramada, I walked into Dillard's department store and asked if I could have a job. I followed a similar pattern to that I had during my interview for my hospitality job, but found myself hired even faster — having experience, I learned, was everything in the working world.

I started the next week. Even though I got discounts on clothes, I hardly spent any money at the store. Being around the newest fashions and helping people look their best was enough for me. Besides, I was now making money from two jobs, and I was enthused about how large my savings for Europe was growing. More than anything, I was proud of myself for being able to turn a potential weakness in my traveler's spirit into a strength of my resolve.

I kept both jobs through the rest of my high school career. While everyone my age was running around spending their money on all the last-gasp fun, I held strong. Finally, as graduation approached, I got permission from my parents, who were proud of my working responsibility, and punched my ticket.

In the summer of 1981, I was seventeen and off to explore Europe. I can vividly remember flying out of New York City and seeing the Statue of Liberty behind me as we soared toward my very first overseas destination. I was too excited to sleep. As morning became clear amid the puffy clouds, I saw red tile roofs of houses, as we landed in Frankfurt Germany. It was my first big trip, and I didn't know it at the time, but it was also the first real spiritual journey I took.

I went alone. Even though I'd saved a good sum, I elected to stay in a hostel so I could meet new people. I survived on bread, cheese, and chocolate bars

— in that order — washing it all down with a Coke, before they changed the recipe. Occasionally I ordered pizza but I steered clear of any pricier restaurants or experiences. I was content with soaking up the essence of the places I visited. I felt I could sleep in the street and survive on the old-world air if that's what it came down to.

That was the gift I felt my spirituality awarded me — even from that very first big trip I felt I could go anywhere at any time and I could survive happily. I discovered the extent of my versatility as I moved on from Germany and arrived in Paris. I swapped my German Deutschmarks for Franks and set out to see the City of Light.

As a boy who was raised Catholic, I found myself drawn to Notre Dame, despite not having set foot in a church throughout my roaming around Germany. From the moment I saw its twin towers across the square, the structure had a magnetism that pulled me in. When I finally stepped inside the cool space, the massive gothic arches swooping alongside the path toward the altar, my jaw fell open. I was moved.

That's how I found myself, a few minutes later, inside the confessional booth for the first time in my life. My parents had tried to get me to go to confession when I was younger but I hadn't seen the point. Out in France, all by myself, I felt a connection with my religious background I had never imagined.

Back then, I believed my travelers spirit had brought me closer to the faith of my upbringing. Now, I realize the two were one in the same. The spirit itself — the very essence of our internal selves —is indivisible. Tourism, in a way, is a byproduct of where leisure met religious pilgrimages in the old days. Connections and adventures are a great reason to travel but there is something more. Though many people still travel for explicitly religious reasons, many others experience spiritual moments when they are away from home. In that way, travel is a kind of spiritual exercise.

Challenged in Jerusalem

"Open your bag sir," the grey uniformed officer asks. His partner stands nearby, a rifle slung over his shoulder and a blue Star of David patch attached to their flak jackets.

People usually think I'm Jewish. They read or hear my last name — Dramberger — and automatically assume they know my racial and religious background. Everyone who travels extensively has dealt with being grouped or stereotyped in some way. Rarely are such assumptions as far off as those who identify me as Jewish when we cross paths. The truth is I'm very much a Christian. I've been that way my whole life. Yet, assumption in travel is not a one-way street. The two go together in other ways too.

This is my first time in Israel. When I landed, what I believed I had ahead of me was a pinnacle spiritual experience. Surely, the birthplace of Christianity and other major world religions is pregnant with religious affirmation and a deepening of faith. I assumed it would be the spiritual journey of a lifetime.

"I said, open your bag sir," the officer reiterates, more firmly this time.

These police weren't like the previous pair who stopped me about an hour before. They had worn more classic garb — light blue collared shirts, navy-blue hats and matching trousers. They had also been more pleasant about the stop and search requests.

His partner swings his rifle from his shoulders, brings it around to his front, and clenches his fingers around the handle.

"Can I ask why I'm being searched," I ask, against my better judgement.

It's never the brightest idea to question police officers in any country, especially not ones as prone to violence as Israel and Palestine.

With a firm response, I come to learn the border guards are conducting routine searches of tourists in Jerusalem. If I have any more questions, they inform me, I can ask them in the comfort of the air-conditioned police station.

I let the officers rustle around my day bag of maps, a guidebook, and camera equipment. The lead officer even flips through the half-full pages of my diary. After a few minutes, they are satisfied and I bite my lip from making a snarky comment about the right way to treat guests.

I'm rarely so irritable, whatever people assume I am. You grow accustomed to minor conveniences as a traveler as well. Still, I had been stopped at least a half dozen times in my first full day in town and the interruptions were taking a serious effect on the spiritual journey I expected to have.

I am only a few minutes from the Old City but feel I need a break. Stop and frisk had exhausted me. I choose a small café called Etz as the location to replenish my excitement.

On the wall above a pair of standard wooden tables are the words, "One life is worth the whole world." The charming café buzzes with activity during the mid-morning rush. Locals and foreign tourists congregate, there are even a few folks working from laptops strewn across the café's dozen tables.

I had been told by friends that Tel-Aviv was like New York City but when I had been there a few days before, I hadn't felt it at all. In fact, this small Brooklyn-like café in the ancient capital is the first place anywhere in the country resembles anywhere in the five boroughs.

I sit down, ordering a small French toast plate and a coffee. My server is friendly and seems to know many customers. When he delivers my steaming cup of Joe outside to my table, I ask if he can venture a guess about why I keep getting stopped by the authorities.

"Well," he said, pausing the way people do when they try not to offend someone. "You do look a little Egyptian."

"Egyptian!" I startle myself with how loudly I repeated him. A few other customers turn curiously my direction. I see one pair of eyes glance at something passing behind me. I spin around to see a passing police car.

When I turn back to the waiter — who appears to be frozen stiff — I can't help but chuckle. I traveled all this way to Jerusalem as a wondering Christian who had been so often confused as a Jew, only to be mistaken for a Muslim. I apologize to the waiter for my outburst and thank him for my coffee.

Through the glare of the window, I examine my bald head and olive skin. I run my hand along my scalp and laugh again. The other diners look at me like I'd lost my mind but I didn't care. When my French toast arrives, I vacuum down all six slices of sugar powdered gooeyness, pay my bill and head into Old Town.

For many years, I had wanted to walk the Via Dolorosa, a popular pilgrimage route for Christians looking to retrace the steps of Jesus Christ on his way to being crucified. There are fourteen different stations, representing places where Jesus falls or is visited by a specific person. I begin my journey at Lion's Gate, which was apparently misnamed when someone misidentified the stone leopards chiseled outside the gate as lions. Apparently, the misassumptions were all around.

At nearly every station of the cross I pass, I also receive my share of visitors. Of course, I am stopped by a few police officers who ask to see the contents of my bag. I also have company in the form of peddlers, desperate to sell me their wares — little trinkets with Christian iconography. One, after my refusing of all his Christian trinkets, shows me his selection of Muslim dribs and drabs. My new mistaken identity as an Egyptian doesn't stop with the authorities and waiters, it seemed.

I do my best to maintain a gracious attitude — I am following in the path of Christ after all — but the frequent interruptions make it impossible. Every time I'm able to close my eyes and exhale into prayer, my pant leg is tugged by a runt looking to help me with a small, fairly priced mini-cross. By the time, I reached the end of the path, I understand in my own way the truth of the Via Dolorosa name — *the painful way.*

Near the Church of the Holy Sepulchre I sit down again, as drained as I'd been at the café earlier and without any cozy coffeehouses nearby to comfort me. I look at the ancient stone walls around me, searching for an explanation for my suddenly lowered expectations. Then, I spot a sizeable group approaching solemnly. Their guide, shoos aside a few peddlers who had pestered me as the group performs the stations of the cross unencumbered. Other folks get out of the group's way voluntarily as if it were protocol. The policemen and the guide even exchange a knowing nod.

For their part, the members of the group appear lost in prayer, thought, and even a few tears. Their parade is one of calm and relaxedness — the opposite of what usually comes to mind when group tours are brought up. The guide stops to utter the occasion fact or historical note, but for the most part even he recognizes the importance of keeping quiet for the visitors to arrive at their own meaning.

It is impossible to tell the religious or racial backgrounds of those in the group. The most progress I make is that they — black, Asian, Latino, Caucasian, male, female, young, old — speak at least some English, or at least nod like they do. Their collectivity allows for no broad strokes, no assumptions to be made by me or any of us outside the group.

There is just a sense of unity and peace within their group but also safety. Once I get over how much of an inconvenience it was to be stopped so frequently, I am able to connect the dots that the officers might not be conducting such searches for the sport of it. Hardly a day passes when news from Israel and Palestine doesn't involve an attack in some fashion. When visiting potentially dangerous places, it's best to travel with someone — like a group guide — who knows their way around and is up to speed on the latest happenings.

As much as I wanted to just want to jot "Israel" wholesale on the short list of countries I don't much care for, I realize that maybe it isn't the shortcomings of the country but rather my own unpreparedness that exacerbated so much of my discomfort while traveling there. It becomes clear to me, lost in the walls of Jerusalem's Old City, that although everyone has their own spiritual path, undertaking certain exercises in faith are not meant to be taken on one's own.

If I ever visit Israel again, I will gladly join a tour group.

Dead in Jakarta

Sweat ran down my back in thick beads as I hustled down a narrow sidewalk careful not to bump the mirrors of the scooters and motorcycles racing past me. The riders had taken the liberty to veer off the main street in their efforts to circumvent a major traffic jam. The sidewalk — which was already not wide enough for the abundance of pedestrians – was further constricted by the impatient motorists, making the whole act of getting from one place to another more complicated than it ought to be. These factors were reason enough for my perspiration but that was before considering the 90-degree weather and 80-percent humidity that made the air itself feel like a soaked rag ready for squeezing.

Running your own business is exhausting, especially when you take a trip to a place like that. There are swarms of imperfect statistics and data that float around online and offline travel advice circles about certain places and their claims to fame. When it comes to megalopolises, one of those murky titles is that of "World's Most Polluted City." How one goes about measuring something like that aside, cities like Mexico City and Guangzhou are often cited as the fullest expressions of filthiness. However, there is another city that consistently comes up: Jakarta.

It's the downside of major development. As countries surge forward to build up economies, they leave a trail of waste behind. Yet, businessmen like myself are consistently drawn to Jakarta because of the magnitude of opportunities in the "sleeping giant of Asia" as the fourth-most populous country in the world has been famously called by economists.

For decades, Indonesia's capital city has drawn rural residents from the country's main island of Java as well Sumatra, Bali, and the approximately 17,000 other islands that lie in its borders. Like other developing countries, this mass migration to cities has been difficult for city planners to account for and as such, these urban areas sprawl and stretch as far as the eye can see as well as the many places it can't. Makeshift residences are fabricated out of salvaged materials. Living arrangements are often unsanitary and unsafe. With even the most basic needs unaddressed, waste management is not the top priority for local and municipal governments.

In short: trash is just about everywhere in Jakarta

It's a fact not lost on a business man as he barrels down a sidewalk toward a meeting a few blocks — but seemingly an eternity in those conditions — away. As I ran along, in addition to the other human beings, I dodged patches of concrete that had been abandoned mid-repair and piles of trash that had accumulated serendipitously. I checked my watch as I came to one pile of pollution my fellow commuters had opted to leap over instead of trying to circumvent. I looked down, hoping to avoid stepping into anything that might muck up my leather shoes before the meeting — Jakarta has its fair share of feral animals — but what I saw below my shoes as I lifted them was something else entirely.

The pollution everyone was stepping over was a body. A dead body.

I stopped mid-leap, causing a human pile-up behind me, with people shouting about their displeasure in languages I couldn't understand. Even if they were speaking English, I doubt I could have heard them. I stood with an unshaken gaze fixated on the deceased human laying on the sidewalk. I wish I could say I'd been wrong. I wish I could say that the figure below me suddenly stirred awake with a little kick, loud noise, or splash of water. The color of his face, along with the dried blood and fluids told me otherwise. There is a certain eeriness present when someone's recently deceased nearby. It's not unlike the feeling you have when standing over a casket at a funeral.

At that thought, my pulse began to quicken. I was outraged. I was horrified.

"Help," I shouted. "Someone needs to help this man."

Aside from a woman who shook her head at me as she scooted by, no one so much as acknowledged me.

"This man is dead," I yelled.

Still, the stream of the living zoomed by toward their various destinations. I looked back down at the dead man's face and tried to find something in it to release me from the responsibility of finding someone to take care of him, someone to treat his body with the dignity I'd expected for all humans. I searched for assurance that this could never be the treatment people I knew received, that it could never be my own fate when my spirit left my physical body.

In my search, I found nothing. There was no respite. Only a nagging sense that I didn't belong there, standing next to a dead body of a man I knew nothing about, in a country I knew very little about, remained. That and the rain, which went from zero to torrential downpour in what felt like a snap of the fingers.

I took a quick gulp of Jakarta's polluted air, made my way around his body and sprinted onward toward the covered walkway that led to the hotel where I had my meeting.

The interiors of a fancy hotel can resemble outer space after an experience like that. Throughout the course of the meeting, I didn't feel like myself. I didn't feel like anyone at all. My spirit was adrift somewhere between the immaculately manicured room where my physical body sat and the drenched megalopolis outside where I felt my soul floated aimlessly.

After the meeting, I passed through a corridor that connected the hotel to a shopping mall. The polished storefronts and reflective surfaces did nothing to shorten the gap I felt between the reality and the surreal. Nor did the industrial strength air conditioning that turned the mall into a refrigerator. I followed the signs toward the public transportation. Jakarta's metro system was under construction and the best they had to offer was TransJakarta, a public bus system with stops built on raised platforms throughout the city. Though the buses travel in separate lanes at times, often they're subject to the same traffic as the rest of the city. I stood shoulder to shoulder with some of the passengers for a while, examining the maps but even though they were in roman script, the language's lengthy words were too much for me to handle.

I reentered the mall and did another lap, hoping for something to draw me in to pass the time until the rain subsided. Instead, the big empty spaces and incredibly small number of shoppers made me feel even more like an astronaut. I bolted out of the chilly mall toward a line of taxis that were picking up Jakarta's wealthy shoppers and their retail hauls. I waited on the roofed platform in the thick outside air for only a few minutes before entering a taxi and feeling the car's cold AC blow against my face as we sped down the driveway toward the crowded streets.

"He was already dead," I muttered to myself. "He was already dead before you got there."

The taxi quickly found itself jammed into the gridlock of Jakarta's rush hour. The rain continued to pour down outside. I tried to steady my breath, extending my exhales for as long as I drew in my inhales.

This went on for a few hours. There was nowhere for the taxis to go. There was nowhere for anyone to go. I'd calmed myself down enough to regain control of my sense of time and space, but now the ever-reliable indicators of the living — fatigue and hunger — were setting in. After I'd remained in the taxi for as long as I could stand, I asked the driver to pull over and paid him for the ride.

The flooding was so bad that opening the door required an extra oomph to push against the rising tide of accumulated water now covering Jakarta's streets. I stepped into this newly formed river without hesitation. My shoes and socks were soaked, and the water level came up above my knees in some places as I waded across the median toward a raised TransJakarta platform that looked like an island in the sea of dark water and yellow cabs.

There, on the platform, I waited with other a handful of other unlucky Jakarta residents, some returning home from work, others from school, a few with some small grocery bags. As I waited there, the vehicles navigating the water sounded like boats. In all my drenched glory, I felt fortunate. Not just fortunate to be alive but fortunate to have the privilege of knowing what it was like not to be soaked on a bus platform day-in-day-out. Fortunate to be able to see the good fortune I had.

I stayed at the bus top long enough until the rain let up. I stopped wondering if the body had been washed away in the storm. Then, I walked back to my hotel.

Shaken Over Afghanistan

On a frigid Helsinki morning, I plopped down into my bulkhead seat directly facing the galley. As I waited for the other passengers to board and settle in, I adjusted in my seat and sifted through the thin reading materials in the thin pocket just below the screen in front of me. I rarely ever look at in-flight magazines but I was curious to see exactly where our flight path would take us.

I used to believe that there were only two types of places in the world: places I'd already been and places I was going to go. As I've grown older, I've learned that there are some regions of the world that will likely never be safe enough to visit during my lifetime. The political atmosphere in these places or other hazards, make visiting more trouble than it's worth. Even more than danger, barriers like cost and not visiting a country on my own terms make these destinations unrealistic.

One of those places is Afghanistan.

I found our flight path at the back of the airline's publication and traced my finger along the glossy pages. I moved through the expanse of Russia, the bulky country of Kazakhstan, and through Uzbekistan. Then I paused and moved my face closer to page. Though the borders weren't perfectly drawn, I could follow our path through the tiny country of Tajikistan and past a northern sliver of Afghanistan.

Though safety in certain Afghan regions has been secured in the past, as well as recent years, there are vast regions of the country that remain wholly inaccessible. It's a safe bet the tourism industries in these areas won't be developed in my lifetime. The border area above the capital Kabul in Northern

Afghanistan, for example, is one of these zones. This is the home of country's mountainous region of Hindu Kush, a mountain range that serves as the border with Pakistan.

Our flight from Helsinki to New Delhi was going to pass right through Hindu Kush. In fact, by my imperfect calculations, we would pass right near Noshaq, the tallest mountain in Afghanistan at just under 25,000 feet. I slid the magazine back into its slot and sat back in my seat. For all I knew, this is the closest I would get to visiting the mysterious and dangerous region.

Hindu Kush is most famous as a passageway. Early on during the historical development of Buddhism, the religion traveled from the Indian subcontinent by way of Hindu Kush. Before moving East toward Asia, Buddhist schools developed in the early centuries after Christ. In fact, the enormous Buddhas of Bamiyan — famously destroyed by the Taliban in 2001 — were built because of the area being a hotbed of Buddhism during this period.

Later, after the Islamic conquest of the region, the passageways through the mountains became primarily used for trading slaves. Once the British empire spread to the Middle East, Hindu Kush served as a geographical barrier they were unable to fully control. The same held true during the Cold War as Soviet forces found the region to be a strategic location but couldn't fully establish itself there. The same problem has persisted since the American predicament with the country began, with Al Qaeda and the Taliban using the region to their military advantage.

A young, female flight attendant with a high-pitched voice and a cute smile reminded our row to fasten our seatbelts then continued down the aisle to tell other passengers to do the same. I strapped in and prepared for the 7-hour flight. I was tired but I didn't want to miss what might be my only chance I had to see this region in person, despite it being from far away. I only wished I'd chosen a window seat

War is the antithesis of travel. The suffocating climate of war sweeps up everything in sight, leaving nothing untouched in its wake. Infrastructure disappears. In places where tribal or racial or religious sentiments are underpinning the wars, the presence of foreigners — often the exact things a country needs to remember its being part of a greater, connected world — sharply decreases. This insularity that war encourages only serves to worsen the problems, making the connections forged between travelers and locals impossible, to say nothing of the adventures.

I'm not a political scientist or a former military commander. War is not my area of expertise. I don't pretend to be an expert in the Afghan, or any other, war. I have no solutions of any kind. However, what I can tell you with some degree of certainty, is that it was the one surefire way to destroy the individual traveler's spirit. Which, for a guy like me, goes hand in hand with the essence of the human spirit itself.

I thought about all of this as our plane took off, climbed to cruising altitude, and our in-flight meal was served. Not quite any definitive arrangement of breakfast, lunch or dinner fare that I could decipher, the offerings consisted of a small fruit plate, a croissant with gouda cheese, yogurt, and a plate of creamed spinach and potatoes with two sausages on top. I ordered a coffee from the kind young flight attendant less because it fit the meal and more because I wanted to stay awake.

"We will now be climbing to well above 26,000 feet according to international flight regulations," the pilot announced. "Please clear your meal and stay seated with your seatbelt fastened."

The flight attendant's chirpiness from earlier sounded subdued when she came around to collect our trays and the garbage. I had her refill my coffee. I drank it and craned my neck over to peer down at the earth. According to the flight map, we were passing right over Afghanistan.

"Please return to your seats," the pilot said. "We are passing over some mountains and there is some fierce turbulence."

I glanced out the window and caught a glimpse of the snowy peaks of Hindu Kush passing below. I swallowed the last sip of my coffee, and wedged the paper cup into the magazine pocket in front of me. No sooner had I discarded the cup than our plane jerked sharply laterally, followed by the pilot's correction the other direction. I saw a glass of cranberry juice splash against the window on the aisle across from us. The liquid had flung out of a passenger's hand.

"Please remove all sharp objects from your possession," the pilot shouted. "I repeat, discard all sharp objects."

The plane shook again and then dove, producing that roller-coaster feeling in my stomach where you feel like your entire insides are going to escape out of your mouth. The plane leveled out, as passengers screamed and those few flight attendants who had remained standing hurried to their seats. Then, it suddenly dipped again, much faster.

"We're going down," someone screamed. "This is it."

I thought about my family. I hoped and prayed they could cope with their loss. The lights in the cabin flashed on and off. In the flashes, my eyes met those of the young flight attendant as she sat across the aisle from me on the other side of the galley wall. She cried silently, clutching the side of her skirt in one hand, and the bottom of the flimsy flight crew seat with the other.

As bad as I felt for her, I couldn't help but thinking about all the people below us. They had lived with the reality of death at their doorstep for decades. They lost people regularly. They had nowhere to go. Those tall, treacherous mountains — the very ones chopping up the high surface winds our airplane was struggling to navigate — was their home. I couldn't comprehend what living in a war was like, but in that moment, I felt the contours of death close by.

I searched for death's face as its figure crept toward us the further our plane fell. I saw flashes of it. I thought I felt it approaching. I rushed to ready myself, my memories and associations freewheeling out of control.

Why now? What could have been different? How will it look on the news? Were we going to join the names and legacies of all those dead on the blood-stained grounds below us? Would our bodies become part of whatever the country would become in the future? What about God?

Then, the plane righted itself.

My thoughts and the screams of the passengers were suddenly sucked up like a vacuum cleaner had swept through the cabin. After nearly thirty full minutes of turbulence, the airplane finally levelled out. There were a few cheers of joys but mostly whimpers that rang out like a collective cry of relief from my fellow passengers.

The woman in the window seat in my aisle slammed the window shade shut. It remained that way for the rest of the flight. I never thought for an instant about asking her to crack it open. I decided I could live without touching the ground of every country on the planet.

Bald in Varanasi

"Really," I said, forlornly. "I'm so sorry to hear that."

I was on the phone with my friend and she had just finished telling me the story about the second child she'd lost to a miscarriage. The tragedy happened a full six months earlier but in the course of our busy lives, and because she had been too upset to talk about it, she'd waited for some time before letting me know.

An hour earlier I'd been fussing in the bathroom with my newly acquired hairpiece. Like any man who has experienced baldness knows, it can be jarring at first. Though I still had traces of my hair intact, I'd acquired a hairpiece on the recommendation of a colleague and was struggling to get it to look right in the mirror before my friend called. My big "problem" that frustrated me earlier didn't seem so big anymore.

"I'll let you know when I'm back," I said, as our conversation wrapped up. "I'm terribly sorry for your loss."

I have no children of my own. It wasn't part of my path. My friend's brother had a family of his own and my friend was ready to start hers. She was just having some trouble. As I prepared for my latest trip to India, one of many I'd taken in those years, she stayed in my mind. The country was a place famous for seekers — usually of the religious variety. India attracted people from all walks of life with all their nagging questions needing answers.

Mine was clear: why couldn't my friend have the baby she so desperately wanted?

I threw my hairpiece in the bag and went to the airport. The second stop on that particular India trip was Varanasi: the holiest of the country's many holy sites, or Sapta Puri. These locations have been pilgrimage sites long before the birth of Christ and were believed to be the associated with various religious masters who'd come to Earth in avatar form. Gods like Vishnu and Krishna, hail from these locations but perhaps Hinduisms best known deity, Shiva, the destroyer of evil and transformer, considered Varanasi his most loved city.

My friend needed some evil destroyed and her luck transformed if she was going to have a child and I decided there was no better intention to keep in my mind on my first trip to Varanasi, with my hairpiece also firmly in place.

Taking a tuk-tuk form the train station, one of the most immediately evident aspects to the city is just how narrow and cramped the place is. Elsewhere in India's more major metropolitan areas, I'd visited districts where small alleys constituted a street but many neighborhoods in New Delhi, Mumbai and Calcutta, had the wide lanes I was accustomed to in the West. Varanasi was a labyrinth the tuk-tuk driver navigated deftly as he wove through the maze, narrowly avoiding the locals and tourists that seemed to come out of every one of the city's cracks en-masse.

I was only scheduled to be in the city for a night and I wanted to spend as much time as I could down where all the magic was happening: the bank of the Ganges river.

Without a doubt, Varanasi is one of the world's most spiritual places. Baba priests wander around with devotees. Even if you're not in touch with your spiritual side, you can't miss the throngs of praying locals and international visitors that roam the small city's streets side-by-side with cows. The scene encapsulates the constant back and forth between seeking and finding that religious folks the world over experience.

Mostly though, Varanasi is known as the place where Hindus go to die. It's ultimately there, beside the river Ganges in North India where friends and relatives bring their loved ones to properly prepare them for the transitionary period between the moment where our life as we know it ceases to exist and the arrival of whatever comes next.

After all, what's more spiritual than death?

Right before I arrived near the river front, I ducked into a small restaurant to have a meal ahead of the long night. I ordered, sat down with a rickety fan nearby blowing slightly less hot air than the absolute sauna outside, and sucked down the last of the bottle of water I'd purchased on the train. The wave of warm air dislodged my recently acquired hairpiece but I quickly restored it. The restaurants other guests weren't patrons so much as onlookers hoping to pass the heat of the day indoors. I smiled at them and they mostly stared at me or up at the small television in the corner broadcasting the latest Bollywood fare.

When the food arrived, it came on a metal platter complete with seven small, deep metal dishes. Each contained a different part of the set lunch menu: rice, a vegetable curry, dahl, soup, yogurt, jackfruit, and paneer. Two different kinds of bread were served, one poppadum and one paratha. I ate strictly with my right hand, careful to leave the left for bathroom use as toilet paper is uncommon in India and water is often preferred even when it is because of the nature of the food waste there is far easier to clean with a spray gun.

I'd finished my meal, taken my trip to the bathroom, and was getting ready to leave when a baba — a guru or a spiritual leader — approached me. I'd been told that interactions with babas were common in Varanasi but had counted on meetings with them down by the river amidst one of the world's greatest religious spectacles rather than in the florescent light and waning breeze from a dying fan at a hole-in-the-wall restaurant.

"Tell me of your troubles," he said.

"I feel fine," I said quickly, stepping around the man. "Enjoy your meal here, sir."

I walked away from the scene, not wanting to be pestered to treat the baba to a meal or get caught up in a conversation that might further delay my arrival at the banks of the Ganges. As I reached the exit of the corridor at the end of the street, I looked back.

"Here," the baba said. "At least rub this before you go."

"Rub what?" I shouted.

"This," the baba said, holding out a small ornament I couldn't make out in the distance between us.

Everyone in the area was watching the interaction to see what I'd do. While my radar for scam artists was up and running because India is full of them, the babas request seemed odd enough to me and his demeanor gave no indications of sliminess. I retraced my steps back to the restaurant.

"Where is this symbol?" I asked.

"You mustn't see it," he said, clenching his fist over mine. "Merely touch it and tell me of your troubles."

I didn't walk all the way back over for nothing. I took the object in my hand. He pressed the smooth, contoured shape snuggly against my palm. I don't know if it was hitting a pressure point or what was happening physiologically but I suddenly felt relaxed.

"Now close your eyes," he said softly. "And tell me of your troubles."

Remembering I'd stored my valuables earlier in a zipped waist belt beneath my shirt, I felt comfortable doing as I was told. I closed my eyes. Then, it all tumbled out of me like a newly functioning faucet.

I told him about my friend. I mentioned her miscarriages. I outlined her desire to have a family and the nature of our relationship. Toward the end of my monologue, I also told him I hated my hairpiece and was embarrassed by my baldness, which for all the thick, long hair he possessed, wasn't a problem I felt confident he could relate to.

"Don't worry," Baba said as I opened my eyes. "Your friend will have a baby on August 14."

"That's weird," I said.

"Why?" he asked.

"Because that's my birthday," I responded, figuring he'd somehow got his premonition lines crossed.

"Well as for you," he answered. "You will not have to worry about your hair for long."

I thanked him, gave a small donation, and walked away feeling somewhat confused. I proceeded on my path down to the banks of river Ganges. With the sun beginning its descent, I booked a short ride out on a boat to the side where the river was flowing and swam with other foreign tourists.

In the distance, I watched people carry dead bodies down to the water on a stretcher. I observed the mixed plumes of incense and smoke from the bodies being burned. The chanting transfixed me to such an extent that when I paddled back to the boat and was brought ashore, I hadn't realized my hairpiece had vanished.

When I told the story to one of my fellow travelers, they laughed and said, "Honestly buddy, you looked ridiculous with that anyways."

I stopped in front of a mirror back on the bank of the river and looked at my reflection. I did look better without the hairpiece but the loose pieces of hair bugged me. I stopped in the first barbershop I saw and asked them to shave my head, laughing about the baba's prediction. I spent the rest of my time in India looking like a monk.

Almost exactly ten months later, my friend had her first baby, a boy, on my birthday, August 14.

Christmas in Fiji

The moment I sat down in the back of the pickup truck I knew it was going to be a tight fit. I counted as six women, four men, and a baby — all of them local Polynesians — climbed up on the rusty bumper and squeezed into the truck bed with me. When I was handed the baby, I started to question the wisdom of my whole decision to join this merry band on the journey to their village on a remote part of Fiji's Vanua Levu island.

Was any of this a good idea?

My trip to Fiji was prompted by the yearly two-week Christmas vacation I received as a tourism professor. I'd spent Christmas all over the world and with relatives across the United States. It seemed the only place I hadn't spent it at that point in my life was a tropical island.

Known for years as Sandalwood Island, Vanua Levu is the smaller of Fiji's two primary islands. I'd spent my first week there visiting the larger Viti Levu after landing in the country's capital of Suva. I enjoyed a dish of Kokoda one evening — a kind of Fijian ceviche made from Spanish Mackerel served inside of a coconut — and visited the country's historic sights to try to understand the country I'd decided to visit. I'd developed the exhilarating habit of buying a plane ticket to a country without yet knowing anything about it and Fiji was no different. Apart from seeing the name on water bottles, I was a stranger to the island nation even if I wasn't a stranger to islands in general.

In my early 30s, I took an around the world trip ticket with eight stops and all of them were islands, though none of them were Fiji. What I found most interesting about island life was how utterly separated you could be from the outside world. After a few days in place like French Polynesia, one of the islands I visited on my island hoping trip, it was easy to forget all about the wider world. It made it even easier when you peered out past the crystal-clear waters and saw nothing on the horizon but more liquid. The world could very well cease to exist and you could very well not care.

But was spending a holiday that celebrated events that happened elsewhere in that world make sense in a place like this?

These were the questions I asked myself when the truck rumbled to life and the dozen of us in the truck bed began the backside insensitive journey toward what I was told would be a Christmas celebration. As a rule, I almost never build up places or experiences in my head when I travel. This is a strategic mental tactic that allows my journey to unfold as it wants to, without me dictating or enforcing some sort of categorical experience on it. I've seen far too many unhappy travelers and vacationers curse bad weather, closed attractions, or other mishaps to expect my trips to be anything other than what they are meant to be. However, when I overheard someone talking about a Christmas they had spent on Vanua Levu at the restaurant where I ate Kokoda on Viti Levu, it kickstarted a chain reaction that had led me to sitting in the back of that pickup truck on Christmas Eve, where I returned the baby to whom I believed it belonged to, and then tried my best to settle in.

After canceling the remainder of my stay at the Viti Levu hotel, booking a ferry to Vanua Levu, and waiting at the designated meeting point — as day turned to night — where the contact had arranged for me to meet his friend from a local village, I was bracing myself for a big letdown. Christmas was a holiday that carried familial and cultural significance for me, but for the first time in my life I felt as though there was a budding spiritual element to the day and my decision to get in the back of the pickup truck was somehow putting that deeper spiritual meaning at risk.

No one wore Christmas attire. None of us sang Christmas carols as we rode along — though the distraction might have helped keep my mind off the pain emanating from my two back pockets. We didn't pass any houses at all, much less any strung with Christmas lights. It wasn't as though I expected everyone in the world to celebrate Christmas in some fantastical way or in the way I had grown accustomed to. I had traveled enough to accept and appreciate the world for the differences — not the similarities — it boasts. Still, I grew upset, crunched up in the back of the truck as the last of daylight disappeared and the only thing I could see was the vague beam of visibility the headlights of the truck offered when I dared lean over the side of the vehicle. I knew my mood was related to my being disappointed by the lack of Christmas spirit I felt. From what I gathered, the people here were just using this truck as transportation to get back to their village from the port. I felt strongly that wherever I was going, the only celebration that would take place would be on behalf of my rear end after the bumpy ride.

I decided to close my eyes. It wasn't sleep I was looking for but something similar. I just wanted to get away and since I couldn't, I decided the best course of action was to temporarily make the world around me disappear. The hum of the truck, the occasional voices of the other passengers, it all slowly faded. I felt a growing warmth growing in my gut as I settled myself, even as my butt went completely numb. When I was finally calm enough, I opened my eyes.

As if by design, the stars had come out. The sky above looked like an enormous firework had been frozen at its point of maximum explosion. Suddenly the world around us was illuminated, the vegetation's bright greenery was a cool indigo in thinned darkness. The baby's eyes were glued to the scene above and after I'd nodded approvingly at a few of my fellow travelers, my eyes returned there too.

When we got to the village, there were long strings of Christmas lights hanging from the palm trees, making the tropical flora glow the same way pine trees did back in the United States. Those familiar holiday sensations that I'd carried with me to all the other Christmases in my life suddenly spilled out. I felt my face contort into a smile so bold I thought it might get stuck that way.

Oh, my Lord!

We stopped and hopped out of the truck. A few of the passengers trailed off for different huts but most proceeded toward the brightly lit larger hut at the center of a clearing not far from where we parked the truck. The man who met me at the dock — who had driven the truck — put his arm around me and let out a whistle as we arrived in earnest to a celebration that was well underway.

We hadn't had so much as a moment to talk when I'd arrived at the dock but now the man informed me that he was a relative of the local I met on the other island. His family had been coordinating this annual Christmas celebration for a few generations, since missionaries had first visited the island. It was one of his favorite moments of the year and from the way the night unfolded, it was clear he wasn't alone.

The village put on a full-blown Christmas pageant. The carols were sung in their local language, many of them with traditional instruments. The actors in the pageant wore grass skirts and typical Polynesian garb. Otherwise, the spirit of the performance was no different than those taking place halfway around the world in the places I'd seen pageants in the United States.

I couldn't believe my eyes. Moments earlier, I felt as desperate for the familiar as I probably ever had in my travels. Yet, the spirit of Christmas had traveled halfway around the world, across more than a few bodies of water, and down a long dirt road as if it had been a trip just across town to Grandma's house. It was a sight I'll never forget and a decision I'll never regret.

Best of all, it instilled a sense of the spiritual side of Christmas I had never expected to come across – especially not in a village in the middle of nowhere on a tropical island that was the equivalent of a speck in the wide world, the way we are just a speck in the history of mankind in the here and now.

Miracles in Medjugorje

"Can I have any volunteers?"

The man stood in front of a group of religious pilgrims. There were middle aged men and women, like myself. There were young kids. There were older folks too and as I looked around, I decided none of them looked like the hand-raising type.

"Volunteers?" he asked again. "Any takers?"

I hadn't traveled all the way to the Balkans to spend my time waiting for other people to step up. I came to Bosnia and Herzegovina to take the leap. If a cross needed to be carried up the side of the mountain, I could do it.

"I'll do it," I said, stepping forward.

"Bless you," the man smiled. "Bless you."

What he hadn't told me when I'd volunteered was that I was expected to complete the journey without a shirt or shoes. Thankfully, I was outfitted in shorts, which would help with the heat. I lathered myself in sunscreen to combat the fierce midday sun that would pass overhead during the 45-minute journey and took hold of the heavy wooden cross.

Medjugorje is a famous Catholic and Christian site because of an event that took place there a few decades earlier. In 1981, six local children said they saw an apparition of the Virgin Mary at a point along a steep path called Podbro. Later, that location became known as Apparition Hill and a statue of the Virgin Mary was erected there to symbolize her appearance.

I'd already visited Apparition Hill earlier that morning. The path leading to it wasn't as challenging as I was led to believe but the site itself was every bit as profound as I could have dreamed. Visitors beside me wept. I saw a man writing a diary entry to himself. Strangers embraced each other, trying to cope with the emotion pregnant in the earth around the area where the Virgin Mary had appeared to the children all those years earlier.

Faith is a funny thing. Everyone needs faith. Even if you are strict atheist, you have faith in your correctness. The essence of spirituality is the *spirit* itself, a vaporous symbol — the presence of something even if you can't physically capture or touch it. I embrace all faiths but I consider myself a Catholic. I can't prove there is a God. Nor can my atheist friends prove that there isn't one. That's why it's called faith.

The expressions I saw of faith at Apparition Hill were unlike any I'd ever seen throughout the glimpses of the spirit I'd seen in my many travels. For us believers, perhaps it's impossible for us to see the spirit as clearly in other faiths as it is when its dressed in the language and culture we're familiar with. For me, having been raised a Catholic, it was impossible not be struck by the fullest expressions I'd seen in Catholicism that morning.

Perhaps, deep down, that's what I wanted to get closer to when I volunteered to pick up the cross a couple hours later. I knew full well I could march to the top of the mountain, lost in the crowd, and have my whatever experience was there for me. Yet, I felt moved to meet my faith face-to-face, and that came in the form of me carrying the cross as Jesus had done. With that in mind, I started the trek up the aptly named Cross Mountain.

The rocks were sharp and painful. The dirt caked onto the sweaty soles of my feet as I hauled the big wooden object up the mountain. I was grateful my feet were callused from years as a distance runner. I stopped only once, about halfway up the mountain, to switch the cross to the other side of my body and then pressed on.

It was by no means the most difficult mountain I'd ever climbed up, nor did it even crack the top ten for physical straining activities I'd taken on as an endurance athlete. All the same, the slight discomforts of the spiritual crucible forced me to address places where I felt my faith was lacking. In the short journey, I couldn't dodge the uncomfortable questions the way I could in daily life. Something about the occasion and location of the short quest emboldened me to approach spiritual weakness head on.

The spirit of a traveler is that of the seeker — one who leaves no stone unturned, so long as the stones are available to turn. What that march up Cross Mountain taught me was that no stone was un-turnable, much as I'd like to tell myself otherwise at different times in my life. When you travel for such spiritual seeking, you can rise to the occasion you've prepared for yourself in way you could never hope to, surrounded by all the creature comforts of home. If I lived at the base of Cross Mountain, why would I ever feel moved to carry the cross up the path? Because it might have been the only trip I ever take to Medjugorje, why not take the plunge?

When it was over and I arrived at the destination at the top of the mountain, the group leader took the cross from me and a woman stepped forward with a scarlet colored rosary extended my direction. Her eyes were sky blue. She had jet black hair and deeply tanned skin.

"Thank you for what you've done here today," she said softly. "Please take this with you wherever you go."

I took the rosary from her and ran my fingers along its wooden beads. It smelled like rose petals. I looked up to ask her what wood the rosary had been carved from to make it smell so strongly of roses, but she had already gone.

We stayed at the top of the mountain for about an hour, praying, meditating, and talking to each other. When we'd all decided it was time for lunch, we walked back down the mountain — far lighter without the cross and far simpler with my shoes the group had hauled up for me. I felt lighter, the earth below me felt soft and forgiving. There wasn't much I could think to want of the world or my trip, but I certainly was very hungry.

Our lunch consisted of grilled fish accompanied by small silver-dollar-sized fried potatoes and a fresh salad. We rehydrated with water and enjoyed a glass of wine. Afterward, we all had some free time, which I spent on the wooden pews inside the twin-towered St. James Church.

That night I joined another group back at Apparition Hill for an evening prayer session. There were thousands of people who gathered in the area to sing "Ave Maria." I locked arms with a few and sung the hymns with them. I was introduced to one of the men who saw Mary appear in 1981, who was only about ten years older than myself. It was a special moment.

Then, when I was conversing with this Italian couple, the evening sky cleared up apart from this one cloud which began rotating in a circular motion.

The stars, which were now coming into view appeared to be turning along with the cloud, almost like a crown was spinning in the sky. I glanced over at the woman next to me, thinking I had lost my mind, and her eyes were as wide as saucers. I asked if she was seeing what I was seeing and she nodded in disbelief. People started screaming and clapping around us and I frantically searched the area for any light technicians that were using tools to make the scene appear. I didn't find anything.

Later, after I got back home, I went to a family party and began telling the story of what I'd seen that night. It was relatively early in the evening. They humored me by listening to everything until I was finished, then they cleared their throat and told me to be careful.

"Let's keep it light tonight Ed," someone said. "Maybe you should keep this story to yourself."

I read other online reports over the following weeks that alluded to what we had seen that night. I wanted to send them to my friends and family members who'd thought I was imagining things. Before I hit the send button, I remembered the rosary I'd been given. I took it out and began to finger the beads as I had when I first received it.

I said a few Hail Mary's and once I was done, I no longer felt like sending anything to anyone. I didn't feel like I had to prove my faith, even in the context of my own experience, to someone else. The comforts of home and the familiarity of friends can put a damper on the profoundness of your travel experiences, especially when they are irregular or difficult to understand, but I realized it was important to maintain a sense of wonder if I wanted a rich spiritual life.

I decided to take the rosary I received in Medjugorje with me wherever I traveled, and I've never left home without it since.

Horror in Nepal

"Get back in your hotel!"

"But I need money," I said again. "I don't have any money."

There were too many barrels to count individually, but I estimated at least twenty men in military uniforms marched past the ATM where I was trying in vain to withdraw Nepalese rupee, and about a third of them were pointing their rifles at me.

"Back to your hotel now!" one shouted.

I did as I was told and began to power walk back toward the mid-range hotel where I was staying in Kathmandu. The streets hadn't quite descended into complete chaos yet, but the atmosphere was like that surrounding an industrial firework before it launches into the air. Nepal's capital was a match strike away from full-scale insanity.

I'd spent the week prior in India on business and wanted to take my first trip to the mountain kingdom of Nepal at the end of my stay for pleasure. The airport had been so wild when I arrived that I had to take a Tuk Tuk. Despite what I'd heard about the country being a more laid-back and easy-going version of the full-scale rat race in India, I'd accepted the fervor at the airport as normal for Nepal. I didn't know any better but when I struck up conversation with my Tuk-Tuk driver, I quickly discovered how uncommon a day I'd chosen for my arrival.

Apparently, Crown Prince Dipendra, the oldest son of the Nepalese Royal Family, had turned an M-16 on his parents and relatives after an intoxicated dispute. In total he killed nine people, injured five, and put himself in a coma.

Bizarrely, the whole affair had turned him into the de facto king of Nepal despite his unconsciousness and murderous behavior.

The Hindu Kingdom of Nepal, as the country was called then, was very much hanging in the balance. As I rode through the city for my hotel, it was as if I was entering a bad disaster movie where the earth might as well have been falling out from under us as we drove, such was the extent of the waves of anxiety, on-edge stares, and general fear setting in among the Nepalese citizenry. It wasn't, at all, what I'd expected.

Nepal had long been a place that conjured images of mountains and meditation. I'd dined at several Nepalese restaurants in the States: where I ate their famous momos — essentially dumplings borrowed from their northern China borders — dipped in creamy orange sauce, the hearty spin they put on the typical Indian samosa — their neighbors to the south, east and west, and slabs of the country's well-known yak chili — perhaps the best tasting, ugly animal I'd ever encountered. With most of the world's highest mountains wedged in their rectangular landmass and these two cultural behemoths on either side of them, I'd expected the country to be an elevated version of the two civilizations with an identity all its own.

The events of the massacre sent any plans I had directly into a tailspin, the extent to which I hadn't felt until I got to the hotel and was told that the gates would be closing in under an hour. If I needed to get anything from the outside world, I needed to get it immediately. Without so much as a Nepalese nickel to my name, I headed straight for the ATM.

After the altercation with the troops in the streets, I retreated to the hotel and approached the frazzled concierge.

"Listen," the English gentleman told me. "We are getting all the guests out of here on the first flight tomorrow morning. There is going to be a coup."

"A coup?" I asked, baffled.

"Yes," he said. "This is biggest Royal Massacre since the Romanovs."

I had long associated Russia with brutality and political scandal. Short sighted or not, what had happened to Russia's royal family almost a hundred years earlier made sense in my understanding of the world. A massacre in a country like Nepal? It was a total shocker to me — as it seemed to everyone rushing to and fro in the hotel.

The concierge recommended I go to my room. I followed his suggestion, completely confused about how I was going to pass the time. I was torn between a sense that there was something I needed to do to help and the crushing reality that there was nothing for someone like me, who knew next to nothing about the place, to hope to accomplish.

On the one hand, it was history in the making. I'd always felt if I hadn't gone into the tourism business, I might have enjoyed life as a reporter on the beat. Though I'd travelled to a great many countries, it was the first time I was around for major political upheaval. There was an excitement to it at first, and I might as well have had a bucket of popcorn next to me when stared out the window, such was the voyeuristic pleasure I was deriving at the expense of Nepal's national tragedy.

When it got dark, the manager of the hotel called every room and invited the guests to the lobby for a meeting. We sat there as he explained to us the extent of the situation. Airlines had ceased operations in and out of the country but they'd managed to charter an Air India plane to New Delhi for us first thing in the morning. He reiterated what the concierge had told me earlier, that they feared there was going to be a government coup and they didn't want any foreigners around to see it who weren't members of the media.

Though I was relieved to know we were being evacuated in the morning before things got bad, for the second time that day I was left to imagine an alternative life as a reporter. I thought about it as I walked back upstairs to my room but by the time I got there and turned on the television, I changed my tune. All over every channel were the images of chaos: people had taken to the streets. They started fires. They made weapons.

Suddenly, I found myself good and scared. I zapped the TV off. I ate a few granola bars I had stored in my backpack from India. I laid in bed and stared at the ceiling for a while trying to calm my heart rate. Then, I began to hear voices outside.

I had drawn my curtains closed as per the advice of the hotel manager but I pulled one sliver to the side and peered out into the night. There were throngs of people marching different directions, shouting things I couldn't distinguish, riding motorcycles. I heard gunshots.

On TV, I'd seen protestors hurl rocks towards police who shot tear gas back toward the crowds. The growing sense that it could happen right there, where the hotel was, didn't seem so far-fetched.

There was nothing to do. No one to call. No exit strategy. If anything were to happen, I wouldn't have known the first thing to do.

I reached into a small compartment in my backpack and pulled out the rosary I'd received in Medjugorje. Its crimson color had given way to a faded, almost burgundy hue. It still smelled of rose petals. I clutched it close to my chest and began to say Hail Mary's.

In the back of my mind I felt I was going to meet my maker. I imagined people bulldozing the hotel. I imaged them going through the rooms and ransacking them, attacking foreigners. I was terrified but I kept praying.

About an hour passed by the time I hung the rosary from my neck and took a break. Nothing about the situation changed. The protestors hadn't quieted down. When I turned back on the TV, the coverage was still showing the riots in the streets. Yet, I felt completely calm. My spirit had found some peace amidst the chaos.

The night didn't pass easily. There was constant danger. I felt things could have gone either way, but I rested easier when I prayed.

As we flew away the next morning, the country still had a long way to go before it stabilized. I was glad to be leaving. In the end, I realized perhaps it was best I wasn't a war reporter.

Part IV: Self

"Why didn't you teach me your mother tongue?"

Is there a more poignant question in the modern American vernacular? In a country full of immigrants, made of immigrants, we in the United States are only now beginning to hint at our own self-realization as a nation. We all wish we knew more about where our ancestors came from. We wish we could speak our native languages. We wish we understood ourselves better.

Who are we, really?

In a way, this is the most *essential* reason we travel. We all want to find out who we are. To do that, we have to discover where we came from. We have to be curious about where we're going. Even once we've learned about our own cultural backgrounds and family histories, we have to try to understand where we fit among that continuum — and indeed the whole of human history — if we are going to become our truest selves.

My father's side of the family was from German descent and my mother's side was from Mexico. Yet, in my family, we didn't like the word Chicano. My mother's side of the family always identified with Spain first. They came over to Mexico City, up through San Miguel de Allende, and finally to Albuquerque. Both of my maternal grandparents were born in New Mexico but when my family moved from San Antonio to Brownsville, Texas, the ancestral Mexican homeland was within walking distance.

It's funny. In my widely-traveled life, the very first time I entered a foreign country was on foot. It was a Sunday. I walked with my parents from Brownsville to Matamoros in the Tamaulipas state of Mexico to see a barber with a handlebar mustache. In what was the first of many trips to his shop, the barber cut my hair, and shaved around my ears. Then, he promptly unveiled an electric device that attached to the back of his hand and he proceeded to massage my head and neck. Afterward, he shook a bit of white powder on my skin, then sent me on my way as my next sibling stepped up.

Afterward, my parents took us to the market square for lunch. For years prior, I had only really conceived Matamoros as the place where our maids lived. My mother would pick them up and drop them off, conversing along the way in a language I only occasionally understood. I watched her order our lunches off a menu entirely in her first-language of Spanish and was impressed with her abilities. I wondered if I would be able to speak the language one day. It was so cool the way she had communicated with the wait staff. It was almost magic.

As we waited for our food, a mariachi trio took the stage. We sat and watched them perform. I looked at the different people and vendors walking past on the street. They sold peanuts, bananas, and corn. There was fresh mango lemonade for sale. Other craftspeople offered their wares to the tourists who had looped a trip to Matamoras into their South Padre Island weekend stay. Kids half my age offered the visitors hats, t-shirts, sunglasses, and whatever else the tourists wanted. The whole atmosphere, though so close to our home, felt intoxicatingly exotic.

When the food arrived, I was blown away about how different it looked from the Tex-Mex I'd grown accustomed to in Brownsville. There was goat cheese on the refried beans. The tacos were smaller and more delicious, according to my siblings. I ordered steak, shrimp, and cherries jubilee for desert because I felt like I was a big deal. Before that I had a savory chicken soup called *caldo*, and enjoyed both a virgin piña colada and a virgin daiquiri before the meal was through.

I knew right away it wasn't going to be the last trip I took across the border. By the time we left the restaurant and walked around the square, which was centered around the gorgeous church, I'd become enamored with the differences such a short distance from my home. I glanced around the local girls in their Sunday best, walking around with each other, talking. The boys, meanwhile, watched them — some walking, some sitting around the square observing. It was like they were two sets of peacocks. Both wanted to see if the other side could work up the nerve to approach and initiate the courting rituals in earnest.

On a deeper level, I felt a vague sense of seeing myself there. I sensed a hint of belonging. My curiosity for Mexico and my mother's heritage was peaked.

When we got back to Brownsville, the family split into our various personal spaces of the house. I was desperate to ask my mother something but I waited until after I'd washed up and everyone else was in bed. We'd had housekeepers for years. They all spoke broken English. I couldn't understand why there wasn't a bigger emphasis on my learning the language of our southern neighbors, the language of my heritage.

"Mom," I said, finding her in the living room reading. "Why didn't you teach me Spanish?"

My mother looked down from her book and watched me for a moment.

"Because Edward," she said. "You didn't want to learn."

I thought about it that night but soon forgot. I was becoming a teenager and I had more pressing concerns. When we'd lived in San Antonio, we'd gone to a private Catholic school. In Brownsville, my siblings and I joined the ranks at the public high school. It was big. There were cliques and crews. Everyone, it seemed, was obsessed with how they identified themselves.

In part because of my budding interest in fashion and my job selling Polo Ralph Lauren, I found myself taking on a classic "preppy-white-boy" modus operandi. Most of Brownsville was Mexican. My siblings and I were only half. Others saw us as the minority, so we embraced it. I didn't want to own my full ethnic background. I wanted to be this white, rich, preppy boy who loved to travel.

"We're not Mexican," I told myself. "We're Spanish. Mexicans are poor people. We're not that."

Matamoras's previous cultural allure for me turned into the same thing it was for so many of the Caucasian American visitors south of the border: a place to party.

South Padre Island was where a lot of teenagers went to cut loose, like the spring break crowd, but in Mexico you could get away with drinking at fifteen and sixteen. We would eat meals and drink. We would go to movies and drink. We would go listen to music and drink. For me, there was a sense of freedom and adventure. I thought I was a big shot.

Eventually we stopped walking across and drove instead. I had a small blue truck. One day, I drove it down and parked near the square. I opened my door to get out and a van taxi came by and slammed into the door and the front of the truck, sending both vehicles spinning out of control. The cops arrived on the scene quickly as the dust was settling. Evidently some people got hurt in the accident and they told me they were going to take me in. I went from feeling I was untouchable to feeling ready to flee back across the border. One of the police had a machine gun hanging over his shoulder though, so I got in the car with them.

I was terrified. I waited in my cell until they gave me a chance to make one phone call. I called my dad. I told him what happened and asked if he could get me out of there. He told me to hang tight. Meanwhile, he made a couple calls to the insurance company and to some friends he had in Mexico. Within the hour, a bribe was paid and I drove my nearly totaled car back across the border to Brownsville.

If my dad had left me in the holding cell a little longer to think about how I wanted to behave when I went down to Matamoras, I probably would have smartened up. As it was, though, I stayed rooted in a white, preppy boy identity, shunned my Mexican heritage, and kept going south of the border to party.

On weekend nights, we started to go to discos. This was the late 1970s and early 1980s. Devo, the B52s, and Depeche Mode were in full force. The music was bumping until the wee hours at the clubs. We drank and smoked cigarettes but I stayed away from the drugs.

One night, my friend got in a fight over some girls he had tried to approach. In the ensuing brawl, we managed to avoid any real damage. To make up for it, another friend suggested he had a better idea of what to do. We grabbed some drinks and followed him elsewhere. He brought us to a motel where older and young women were waiting outside. My friend who'd been chasing the women felt up to it and he paid for two girls to join him in a room. He looked over at me to join him but something changed then. There was something about the situation that grossed me out — driving down to Mexico just to party and take advantage of these women. It was too much. Matamoras was starting to feel like home and this wasn't how I would behave at home, so why would I do it at someone else's house?

Later that night, my friends wanted to drive home. I knew we were too drunk. We found another hotel nearby and decided to stay the night. My parents were reasonably lax with how I spent my time, seeing how dedicated I was to my part-time jobs, but I knew they would flip if I didn't come home. Still, my experience earlier in the evening and the one problem I already had with vehicles in Mexico was enough for me to prefer upsetting them instead of risking the drive.

In the end, they were livid. I told them truth. We were drunk and we didn't want to cross the border. They calmed down eventually, asking me to call them next time, but in my mind, I was done acting a fool in Matamoras.

Later in life, after I graduated high school, started traveling the world, and became a Tourism & Hospitality professor, I briefly moved to San Miguel de Allende, the city in Mexico where my mother's family last lived before immigrating to New Mexico. Although I could get by conversationally, my Spanish wasn't excellent. To an extent, it was true that I didn't *need* Spanish to get by — neither did I need any of the foreign languages for most of the countries I visited prior.

Yet, during my time in San Miguel de Allende, I got to look back on the shortsighted young man I was growing up in Brownsville. As I walked through the colonial city, observing the beautiful architecture, I passed poets, artists, writers, and painters. I wondered what it would be like to talk to them about their work. I wondered about what was lost by not rooting myself in my true mixed identity.

On a stroll one day, I even went so far as to regret parts of my youth until I came home to find the woman who ran the residence house where I stayed, standing outside in her sun dress. She was screaming something at someone passing by. At first, I thought they were having an argument but when they both started laughing I found out it was all in jest. In that moment, I realized that maybe not learning Spanish was the lesson I needed so I could be more appreciative and respectful of everything in the big wide world that I would never know.

The path to self-realization is the never-ending journey. It's populated with twists, turns, hurdles, and forks in the road. Sometimes we don't have the stomach to keep going. Sometimes we even give up. For the truly travel-loving amongst us though, we know that any break is only temporary. We understand that even though our lives will end, the story will go on forever, and writing the chapters that have been assigned to us is the principal task at hand for the self-aware. After all, a border crossing might be only a short walk away at any moment.

Speaking Out in Doha

The shiny floors are familiar. The affirming beep when you slide your card against the ticket stall is too. Even the narrow glass corridor feels like any other metro station I'd visited the world over. And yet, by the time I step aboard my first subway car in Dubai something is off. The squeaky-clean interior contains only a handful of seats, so plush and padded they look like they would fit better in a Maserati than a metro. When I hear the Arabic announcement give way to the English translation — "please stand clear of the closing doors" — I still don't realize I am in the wrong place.

As is my protocol for visiting any region, I had mentally prepared myself for the forecasted cultural differences. The itinerary for a long-overdue business trip to Dubai and Doha included, among other activities, dinner at the world's only seven-star hotel, an excursion into the vast desert, and lodging at the Four Seasons. It's common knowledge to anyone with an internet connection that these cities have redefined the luxury experience. Before I even arrived in the country, the region's trademark extravagance had already taken hold.

At the time of my visit, a client of mine was one of the famous Gulf airlines. This meant my usual seat in coach was upgraded to business class. I had some impressive first-class experiences before, so despite the airline's reputation for opulence, I felt prepared. How incredibly wrong I'd been. The business experience was singular in its luxury. You get your own suite. You don't even have to see the person beside you, with a divider one convenient button-press away. Forget complimentary champagne, you can order any drink that fits your fancy. There are snacks. There are smoothies. You consume whenever and whatever you want.

I basked in the opulence during my half-day flight and when I arrived I felt rested, ready, and — for lack of a better word — like a rich guy. I retrieved my carry-on— which had been stored alongside the finest designer bags belonging to my fellow business class fliers — and meandered through the impeccably dressed masses shuffling around Hamad International Airport in Doha. At the luggage claim, men donned the long white traditional garb — a Thobe — adorned with the customary Arab scarf, called a Ghutrah. Women wore Abaya dresses with various head wraps including the Burquah, Hijab, and Shayla. Locals and international travelers alike moved with an air of entitlement through customs. My eyes only adjusted back to reality from the sparkly surfaces and bright lights of the airport interior when I saw a poor man wandering in the airport welcome area near me.

"Excuse me," he said, calling out to passersby in an Indian-accented English. His clothes were worn but not ripped or shredded. His dress was the standardized plainness of a construction worker, without the sturdy shoes I was used to seeing in the West.

"Sir," he called out toward a pair of men on with cell phones pressed to their ears. They avoided so much as acknowledge his presence, instead swerving around him like he was a pothole in an otherwise pristine highway.

I am accustomed to people watching. It's a favorite pastime of mine, whether I'm traveling for connections, adventure, or the spirit. Something else drew me to observe this man, something deeper inside me — spurred, no doubt, by the way his presence crashed me back to more earthly matters after the entirely heavenly experience I had in the skies.

"Please, sir," the man said to a Qatari gentleman who's rushed state nearly caused a collision between the two.

"Excuse me," the Qatari shouted.

"I am looking for the elevator to the departures," he stammered.

The Qatari sneered. I began a slow walk toward the scene.

Knowing this trip was on my horizon, I had been following the news from the region closely. Despite the FIFA soccer organization's corruption, the 2022 FIFA WORLD CUP was still scheduled to take place in Qatar. A dozen stadiums had to be built or renovated to host the tournament. Like other ambitious construction projects, developers chose to hire cheap migrant labor from places like India, Nepal, and Bangladesh. I'd scrolled through more than a few news reports of mistreated workers and even deaths at and around these construction sites.

"Don't talk to me," the Qatari ordered, looking at the man like he was a disease-ridden street dog. "Don't you even address me."

While there was no way to tell if this man was one of those mistreated workers, my feet made the decision to act for me. As a rule, I am especially cautious when I travel. I'm on guard. No one ever wants to go to prison but especially not overseas. Generally, I avoid confrontation of any kind abroad but over the years I've also learned to trust my instinct. I have faith in myself to do the right thing.

""Do you need help?" I asked the poor fellow, who had clammed up after the berating.

"That's not cool, what you're doing right now" I turned to the Qatari. "This is your country."

I wish I could say he took a deep breath and apologized. He did not. He stomped away in a huff. I'm glad I can say he didn't head toward the police station. He could have told the police the poor fellow and myself had done something terrible. We could have been in serious trouble. In the end, I simply helped him find the elevator he was looking for and moved on.

Over the course of my visit in Doha, I witnessed more evidence of the divide between the classes. There were people with cardboard boxes for homes within walking distance for hotels where every floor had its own butler. I saw TV's on the mirrors in the bathroom at these places and around the way I saw a group of men who lived without a toilet or running water.

By no means is the problem unique to the Gulf region. I had explored shanty towns in other destination countries, even tropical ones like Indonesia and Brazil. Though many of these places do their best to keep the two worlds separated, crossover is inevitable. The favela shantytowns surrounding Rio de Janiero cascade down some of the lushest hillsides, near the city's most pristine beaches. Clashes between the classes are unavoidable for locals and tourists alike. In Qatar and the United Arab Emirates, because of their famed penchant for the extravagant, the differences are simply that much more jarring.

A few days later, I visited Burj Al Arab — the seven star Dubai hotel that's designed to look like a sail fin. It took me a month to get a dinner reservation. I had accompanied a delegation from Houston for a meal that included steak tartar, caviar, intricately chopped vegetable dishes, locally caught fish and deserts that rivaled the Dubai architecture in their immaculate construction. Everything, it seemed, had to be paired with champagne.

The final bill was $9,000.

It was hard, again, not to feel like a rich guy. In Dubai, I'd watched people slide down an indoor ski slope. There were ATM's that distributed gold bars. I witnessed myself making a hierarchy of my preferred excesses. I'd been to the real Venice in Italy and was surprised to say I enjoyed the gondola ride through its Dubai counterpart more than I ever had the tackiness of the Las Vegas replica, The Venetian. Though I'd been on trips where the budget was no issue and others where it was more like a fraction of a shoestring. Never, in any trip, had I felt so lavish as I had when the automobile-sized bill arrived at our table, which puts us right back in the fancy Dubai metro car the very next day.

I sit there, in the plush chairs for two stops, completely dumbfounded before I am finally approached by a man in uniform. Despite my experience at the Doha airport, my absurd dinner, and my various inner dialogues that followed, I have not prepared myself adequately for the gulf between classes in the Gulf. I am told, politely, that I am in a gold class metro car and that the section I paid for, the silver class is behind me. It seemed, even the public transportation here — society's great leveler — is split into haves and have-nots.

Once I moved back a car and took a seat on the standard plastic bench chairs you see in subway systems the world over, I feel, for the first time since I arrived in the region, relaxed.

Longing in San Francisco

There is a saying that goes, "The coldest winter in my life was a summer in San Francisco." An overstatement, though it may be, the sentiment that the weather in the Bay Area can be incredibly unpredictable — and often very cold — is one that you'd be hard pressed to hear argued wrong, even by even the staunchest San Franciscans. When I arrived in the city after I'd just finished my MBA, however, it was as beautiful a spring day as I could have imagined and I had yet to hear this famous quote about San Francisco's weather.

After getting things squared away at my new apartment, I took a walk in the North Beach neighborhood. I started at the Embarcadero, continued through Pier 39, and ended at Fisherman's Wharf. It was a weekday afternoon and the city was humming along quietly. There was a palpable energy I'd imagined must have resembled the vibe that propelled the great many men who migrated to San Francisco during the Gold Rush era. I ate a steamy clam chowder bread bowl at a hawker stand toward the end of my stroll and enjoyed some of the most delicious chocolate I'd ever had at Ghirardelli Square to top it all off.

Every day that followed, I took similar adventures to the city's various neighborhoods. I enjoyed Mexican food and murals in the Mission. I delved into the history of Haight-Ashbury and retraced the steps of counterculture revolutions there. I admired the Painted Ladies and the masterpieces at the Museum of Modern Art. Everywhere I turned, the city had food unrivaled in any city I'd ever been.

I was head over heels in love with the place in only a couple of days.

About a week after my arrival, I took a work trip to Sydney Australia. It was one of the first times in my life I wasn't thrilled to be jetting off to a destination. The plane took off and I looked down at the beautiful Golden Gate Bridge as we sped off into the great Pacific Ocean, I felt almost sad. I was really just beginning to scratch the surface of San Francisco — there was so much to see and do. Even though I'd only be gone ten days, it was jarring to pump the breaks on my whirlwind tour of my new home city. It felt almost wrong to leave it right then.

When I arrived in Sydney, it was Autumn. I instantly wished I was back in San Francisco, where the flowers were just starting to bloom and the citizens were jutting out into the streets for the first time since winter. In Sydney, it was as though the fun had just ended and people were getting ready for the colder winter months. The purple blossoms from the famous Jacarandas that bloom in the spring months had long since fallen.

Once I accepted I would be back in San Francisco soon, I put my head down and went to work. Though I spent most my time in Sydney running between conference rooms and business meals, I did find a couple hours each day to explore the city with the plan to use the two full days at the end to dive deeper into what peaked my interest. I'd been there once before with my father, but visiting the city on my own afforded me to travel as I most prefer: by the seat of my pants. I was whimsical, I followed my intuition, and I changed course at a moment's notice.

In the Harbour City — as Aussies famously call their capital city — I visited museums and zoos by day, restaurants and lounges by night. What I'd discovered was underwhelming to say the least. Everything I saw, I compared to San Francisco. The restaurants weren't as good. The museums weren't as interesting. The sights were less impressive. I burned the first few days in town completely lost in this haze of the grass across the sea in Northern California being far greener than whatever New South Wales had to offer.

It wasn't until I was complaining about such differences to some locals at the work conference that I started to change my tone. Instead of trying to argue for their city, they agreed that San Francisco was an amazing place, but offered to take me out on their town.

Fort the next few days, we enjoyed dinners together at all the city's hotspots. The food was good but above all else, I found the city's residents to be gorgeous — some of the most beautiful people I'd ever laid eyes on in all my travels. I felt like my neck was sore from spinning around to witness the good-looking passersby I saw roaming the streets.

The day before I had to fly back to San Francisco, I'd finally stopped thinking about how rapt I'd been by the Bay Area, such was my new-found affinity for the Harbour City across the Pacific. I was invited by some friends to visit Sydney's iconic Bondi Beach for a swim.

"Isn't the water too cold to swim this time of year?" I asked.

"Not at all mate," my friend said. "If you want to take a dip in the ocean you can but we're going to Iceburgs."

Come to find out, Icebergs is a swimming club, which originally opened in the 1920s and overlooks Australia's most famous beach. I was nervous, because of the well-known aptitude of Australian Olympic swimmers. Once I arrived, dipped into the water and found a lane, however, I felt completely at ease to take a few laps in the amber Autumn sunlight.

The other swimmers were friendly and I made conversation with several members. When I asked how often they came to Iceburgs, most said they came weekly. As we spoke, I heard the ocean waves crash against the rocks below and watched a fan of droplets delicately spray over the railing into the pool's edge, and I realized I'd never seen a pool so beautiful in my life.

When we'd finished exercising, we showered, changed and headed into the club's famous restaurant for a bite to eat. Overlooking the pool below and the beach behind it, we enjoyed a white table clothed meal beginning with a pot of black mussels in a white wine, tomato, and chili sauce. I ordered a filet of grilled barramundi in an herb and garlic butter sauce as my main. One of the locals was an expert in Barossa Valley wines from Australia's southern coast. We tried a shiraz, which I'd never even heard of, and was completely awed by its complex but gentle flavor.

Afterward we walked the small, half-moon shaped sand bar. I listened to them tell stories in their jovial vernacular. By the time I got back to my hotel, I admitted to myself that I'd been charmed to pieces by Sydney. The next morning, I boarded my flight back to San Francisco and was sad to see the Harbour City and the Opera house fading into the distance as we flew the other way back across the Pacific.

A thick fog obscured all but a few of the city's building when we landed in the Bay Area. I took a taxi home and could hardly recognize the place from the one I'd left behind. I slept early and woke up the next day, hoping to return to the place I'd been before I went to Australia.

What followed wasn't just a single cold afternoon, but a hefty collection of them that stretched into the summer. Tourists overran the city. The bread bowls were soggy. Lines for the restaurants grew long and reservations were impossible to land. The city's seven square mile space suddenly felt suffocating.

Worst of all, the city's many beaches were too cold to swim in. The water was freezing, even in the summertime. Only maniacs went in without a wetsuit and I was beginning to grow tired of how many people were out of their mind in the city. Days would go by where everyone I passed wanted to desperately hang onto some part of the 1960s.

I longed for Sydney. I wished I could see the warm and attractive faces I met there, instead of the gruesome and extreme personalities I met in San Francisco. I dreamt of Icerbergs swim club, not the ice-cold waters of the Bay Area.

I said as much to the new friend I'd made in Sydney one day on the phone.

"Wait, wait, wait," he stopped me mid-way through my complaining. "When I first met you, all you could talk about was San Francisco. Loads of my mates here would die to be in your shoes there — what happened?"

Just like that, I realized the greatest danger in any heavy traveler's life: the sensation of always wanting to be somewhere else. It was one thing to look back fondly on a trip or anticipate a forthcoming adventure, but it was quite another to bask in the risky business of comparing two places to one another.

Certainly, Sydney and San Francisco — two of the world's greatest cities — each had their merits. It was when you tried to compare them that they both began to look unattractive. Perhaps these sorts of comparisons are just human nature: we do the same thing with past relationships or even dishes at a restaurant. The reality, however, is that no two things are alike. It takes a measure of self-awareness and restraint on the part of the heavy traveler to abandon these sorts of comparisons.

I realized, with the phone wedged in between my cheek and my shoulder at my kitchen window in San Francisco, that the grass is always greener on the other side if that's where you've directed your gaze. Just as I wrapped up the conversation, I pushed aside the curtain and saw a sight I hadn't seen since I got back to San Francisco from Sydney a week earlier. A band of sunlight was stretching up the street. Almost on cue, I saw a fellow San Franciscan at the apartment across from me, looking out the window with his phone between his shoulder and his ear.

For the rest of that day, I wondered where he'd just returned from.

Overdoing it in Bangkok

I admit it, I was tired. For the fourth week in a row, I had jetted off to a destination a few hours from my home in Pattaya, Thailand for a weekly seminar. The last time around, it was Singapore but prior to that I'd flown to Denpasar, Kuala Lumpur, and Phnom Penh. The proximity of Bangkok to these and other Southeast Asian cities was a major motivation for my moving to Bangkok in the first place. My plan was to see everything and do everything on both a personal and professional level in the region. If I'm being totally honest, however, the go-go-go pace had left me not just tired but utterly exhausted.

I'd gone to the Lion City for a round of training sessions with the local tourism industry. The young professionals were eager to learn and that motivated me to give my all during every session. The industriousness of these workers was reflected in the culinary sensations in the city, where I roamed in between sessions. Of the twenty Michelin star restaurants in Singapore, one included a hawker stall, where an expert chef cooked the city's famous Chicken Rice dish for less than $2 – that's ten to a hundred times less than food at the other Michelins star places. It really deserved to cost more, the way the succulent meat slid off the bone when you bit into one of the crispy, ruby bronzed legs. You can be as tired as imaginable but with food that good, for that price, that close by, there was no way I was missing out.

Singapore had gone well from a business and culinary perspective, but I was exhausted before I ever even arrived. The night before I'd left, I attended a wedding I'd been invited to in Bangkok. The event took place on one of the city's many rooftop dining spaces. This one specialized in Italian food — so much so that even the owner and all the staff spoke fluent Italian. The food was superb, as was the wine, and the whole affair was one of the more beautiful and well-executed events I'd ever been to, wedding or otherwise. Bangkok itself was such a draw for fun, work, and excitement that I hardly needed to leave the area. Yet, my travel-bug had grown into a full-blown monster and I couldn't resist tacking on a trip to Singapore even if it came on the heels of the Bangkok wedding.

Suffice it to say, I was a special sort of drowsy when I got off the plane at Bangkok Airport and made my way to the shuttle to take me the 60ish miles to my flat in the seaside resort town of Pattaya. I paid for the fair, crawled up the stairs, set my travel case down on an empty seat so I could slide my carryon onto the overhead shelf, found my seat nearby, and plopped into it. My eyes fell shut before I so much as buckled my seatbelt.

It wasn't until the driver hit the brakes, sending me smashing into the seat in front of me, that I regained consciousness. I wanted to know how long we had left on the ride and patted my pocket to find my phone. It wasn't there. I reached into my jacket pocket. No dice there either. In fact, neither of these pockets had my wallet either.

Where is everything?

I remembered then that I'd left my travel case — with my passport, my wallet, and my cellphone – on a vacant seat when I first entered the shuttle. I frantically stood up and wobbled down the row of seats, the other passengers turning to watch the goofy foreigner with the bravery to stand up in the unpredictable Thai traffic. I got to the chair where I thought I left the case but it was gone.

Then, I did something I'd never done in all my travels: I had a full-blown freak-out.

Maybe it was the exhaustion. Maybe it was the fear. Maybe — much as an experienced traveler like me hated to admit — it was that feeling of being in a country where you don't know many people, don't speak the language, and don't know how to take care of a problem. Whatever it was, it felt hopeless and I began to cry.

"What happened?" I heard a voice say.

I tried to stop the flow of tears and sobs but couldn't make out anything in the dark, wetness in my line of sight.

"What can I do?" the voice said again.

I brushed my eyes across my sleeves and opened them to see a young woman standing up in the aisle beside me. In perfect English, she explained she worked at the airport's Versace shop. Then she asked again, what happened. I told her about the missing phone and money — and then the missing passport.

Like it was not the first time she'd dealt with that sort of thing, she dialed up the US Embassy on her phone but it was 10 PM and the office was already closed. She told me we wouldn't be able to do anything until Monday morning. It was Friday night. Despite her kindness, this only threw me into a bigger mess of emotion.

The outburst promoted her to squeeze beside me and head up to the bus driver. The two of them exchanged a short conversation in Thai. A few moments later, the driver pulled over on the side of the road. The lights came on. Among the mostly Thai passengers, there were a few German tourists, another American, and a pair of Aussies. Then, the two of them — the Versace woman and driver — stood up to address the passengers. First, the driver spoke in Thai, then the woman translated in English.

"Whoever has this man's belongings," they said, pointing at me. "Please return them to him now."

I dried my eyes and turned around to see if anyone came forward. The German's groaned and said something to each other but neither moved. Many of the Thai passengers didn't so much as look forward. One of the two Aussies remained asleep during the whole affair.

"Alright," they continued. "We are going to Pattaya bus station but first we will be stopping at the police station."

I was stunned. I couldn't believe the driver was going to put all the passengers through this much of an inconvenience because of my negligence. I figured it may have been a bluff to see if the perpetrator would come forward. When they didn't, the driver jumped back to his seat. The woman sat up near him as they continued to talk as we got back on the road.

To my surprise — and relief — the next time we pulled over it was to the Pattaya Police Station. I felt like a fool for what had transpired. I was embarrassed that I'd cried but I was also eager to get my things back.

The officer got on the bus and pointed to the girl and I, motioning for us to get off. We did as we were told and he began to interrogate everyone else on the bus. I waited patiently outside, trying to guess who it would be.

A ladyboy, his sister, and woman who I assumed was his mother, came down the stairs after a few minutes. This was the group I'd suspected. There was just a way they avoided looking at us that screamed *guilty*. They walked past us and I watched them throw the black case against some nearby bushes. The officer saw them, as I had, and hurried over to accost them.

Shortly thereafter, I was handed my black case. All the family had taken was the Thai money I had, which amounted to no more than 900 Baht, the equivalent of $30. Oddly, I had a couple thousand U.S. dollars in cash in the case which they'd left behind, along with my credit cards and my passport.

The police asked me if I wanted to press charges against the family. I told him the sister and the woman could go, but letting the ladyboy — who had thrown the case into the bushes — off the hook just like that, seemed wrong. The police agreed and they took him away for a three-day stay in the Pattaya jail.

The whole thing was exhausting but by the time we got back on the bus, and made it to the bus station, I felt much better. The woman who helped me insisted in giving me a ride to my flat and I was happy to oblige. On the ride home, we talked a bit about what I did and she explained how she learned her English and professional skills from a tourism professor like me.

For so many reasons, the experience felt like I had come full circle. In countless training sessions and classes, I had stressed to students and professionals how it was so important to keep your cool during the stressful situations that travel often brings on. Having a cool head is important in life in general, but it can be a make-or-break disposition in the tourism world. Finally, the well-traveled teacher — who thought he could be a traveling superman, immune to the dangers of pushing the envelope too far — had become the student.

I'll never get to thank the tourism professor who taught that young woman, but I was left with a renewed appreciation for both my profession and myself as an individual traveler.

Wising Up in Genoa

The room stunk like a dirty jock strap. That's the nicest way I can put it. It reeked. The stench was so fierce it was painful to inhale. I'd heard hostels could be breeding grounds for some of the foulest smells in the hospitality industry, but I didn't expect to be hit full force on my very first overseas trip.

I was still a teenager at the time, unwise to the ways of the world, unsure of the flimsiness of life, and how very little time we all have. Still, I had brought with me on that first European journey, the confidence and self-assuredness that only youth can bring. Even with so much I didn't know about the world, I was sure of myself and I knew that if I didn't open a window, all hell was going to break loose.

"Hey, man," another occupant of the six-person dorm shouted to me after I'd cracked it open and crawled back to bed. "Why don't you leave that window shut? It's cold out."

"I don't care how cold it is," I said. "We're all going to die if we don't get a little fresh air in here."

Without answering me back, the perturbed occupant rose from his lower bunk and slunk over to the window, slamming it shut. I didn't look up to see who it was. I already knew by the way the bed shook when he stood up and returned that it was the Ohioan.

I'd met my Midwestern traveling companion — the first one I ever had, it being my first overseas trip and all — in Paris about ten days before. He was a blue-collar worker who'd saved enough spare cash in Columbus to run around Europe the whole summer. He was a full decade older than me but it was also his first time taking the fabled "backpacking around Europe" trip so many young travelers fantasize about.

We got on well enough, but I suspected our traveling together was more about company and splitting costs than our being kindred spirits. This thought first came to me after I noticed a pattern of him delving out different kinds of traveler wisdom to me when we came across various situations on the road. He'd explain to me what certain signs meant in French, even though he didn't speak the language. He'd tell me why a certain European breakfast customs differed from American ones, with a tone of longing in his voice. He offered to show me how to roll a European-style cigarette, making a mess of it in the process.

I quickly surmised the truth in his words. The reality was he knew no better than I, having never been to Europe himself either. In fact, the frequent experiences I had of youth traveling into Mexico probably put me higher on the savviness totem pole than him. The more time we spent together, the further I felt justified in my assessment. Yet, I had no intention of ever delving into the right or wrongness of any of his advice or observations. I was perfectly content with him having his experience and me having mine.

We continued to travel together by train. After Paris, we rode to Geneva. Then, we wound through the famous Swiss mountains, down into Milan, and finally to the historical port city of Genoa.

We planned to use the city as a base to explore the Italian Riviera along the Mediterranean Sea, like the stunning coastal towns of Cinque Terre. I was also drawn to Genoa because it was the birthplace of Christopher Columbus. Even though I wasn't feeling a kinship with my novice traveling companion, I did feel a connection to the famous explorer and wanted to know more about where he came from.

Our first day in Genoa was spent near the sea, watching the fishermen, the boats and swimming in the calm waters of the Mediterranean. We splurged to try the city's famed mussels — drenched in a wine and spicy tomato sauce — then filled the rest of our stomach space with pillows of focaccia bread in oil and pesto. By the time the sun was setting, we found a couple of cheap bottles of wine and meandered our way through the narrow, hilled alleyways toward the city center.

When we arrived at the massive Piazza de Ferrari — the center of the city now as it was back when Genoa was the main port of the Roman empire —

the expanse of the square took my breath away. The fountain sizzled in the center. Citizens and tourists mingled in little groups as businessmen shuffled home from their offices overlooking the stunning expanse of the plaza.

We found a pillar to rest our backs against and sat down with our wine, as we had in other cities in Europe, to take it all in. Perhaps it was that he'd been as enchanted by the city as I was, but my Ohioan companion hadn't delved out any "travel lessons" for me since we'd arrived in Genoa. We'd enjoyed the splendor on equal footing without paying much mind to our gulf in age. My tactic of keeping my mouth shut had finally earned me the right of not being pestered.

We were approached by a few vagrant-looking young boys in tattered clothes. It wasn't the first time we'd been singled out and asked for money or food from the local impoverished youth. This time, perhaps galvanized by the wine and our pleasant experience of the day, the Ohioan stood up and greeted them with a smile. They had a conversation I couldn't completely hear, after which the children scurried away excitedly.

It had usually taken us nearly half-an-hour to rid ourselves of people asking for money at other stops on our journey. We always told them we were traveling by a shoestring and didn't have much to spare but that didn't deter them. This time, however, the children had vanished so quickly I was desperate to know what his trick was — perhaps he finally did have some travel savviness to glean.

"Alright," I said, setting my bottle of wine down on the cobble stone plaza. "What'd you say to get them to scram like that?"

The Ohioan snickered and plugged his lips with the rim of his wine bottle and titled his head back.

"C'mon," I asked again. "Tell me."

Before he could respond the kids returned. Each of them held out a plastic cup in front of us. As he began pouring the remainder of his wine into their cups, his secret offer became evident: free alcohol.

I watched as my bubbly companion cheered and drank with the boys. They swirled around him and I started to get nervous. I quickly checked to make sure my belongings were secure, then I stood up. Not once had I so much as suggested I might be more travel savvy than my companion since the day we met but the pretense had gone on long enough. It was time I spoke up.

"You better watch it," I whispered in his ear.

One of the boys hugged him, feigning gratitude, but I suspected something else. Then, the boy reached toward me.

"Get the fuck away from me," I said, surprised by my own directness.

"Watch your pockets," I said walking away, not willing to risk hanging around the sly kids.

I edged my way closer to the fountain where there was some empty space. I inhaled a breath of the misty air and exhaled. I hoped I'd spoken up soon enough but as the Ohioan approached after a few minutes, it was clear I hadn't.

"Those bastards got my wallet," he said.

Having spent so many days with him in my ear about what I should and shouldn't do, how I ought and ought not to travel, I had been completely frightened off speaking up. I didn't want to come across as a know-it-all or a prima donna. I learned that night, so early in my traveling life, that sometimes being a self-aware traveler means you have to interject, even if it risks temporary discomfort.

A few days later, during that first night in the stinky hostel, I was determined not to let others suffer greater costs because of temporary minor discomfort. I waited for him to crawl back into his bed before I leapt again from my top bunk, with all the limberness of youth, and cracked the window open again.

"Can you close the window," a different fellow from the Ohioan, who'd initially opposed my open-window policy, moaned. "It's so cold."

I sat up in my bed. I decided then and there that I didn't want to waste another instant of my traveling life by pussyfooting around an issue. It was time to trust myself. It was time to insist.

"Look," I shouted. "We're keeping the window open goddammit, and that's all there is too it."

The whole room went silent. All I heard was the sound of sleepy bodies adjusting on noisy mattresses and pulling blankets over their heads. Slowly, but surely, the room began to smell better and I could sleep.

Paying Respects in Borneo

The chief held out the jar and shook the murky contents inside indicating I should grab it. I scanned the other unfamiliar faces sitting cross-legged on the straw mat in front of me, their expressions ranged from the moderately curious to the visibly downtrodden to the outright distraught. Not wanting to lose face in front with the village chief, who'd offered to host me for the evening and who's tribe — the Iban — I knew to at one time be feared for their head-hunting predispositions, I took the jar and took a healthy gulp of the mysterious liquid inside.

The only thing more bizarre than attending a funeral for someone you never knew is attending one as the first thing you do in a place you've never been. That was the exact situation I found myself in after being invited to visit the Malaysian state of Sarawak on Borneo island. Only a few hours earlier, I had left my cozy hotel in the charming capital city of Kuching at the invitation by the ministry of tourism after they heard me speak at a conference for eco-tourism.

Typical of my approach to invitations to places I've never been — and that few foreigners are ever invited to stay — I gladly accepted. What that acceptance entailed was a rowdy jeep ride for a few hours over some mountainous jungle before we were greeted by a small wooden canoe at the mouth of a river. I hopped on with just my backpack and my guide as the morning gave way into noontime.

A short while after our arrival at the village dock and a foregoing of usual pleasantries, my native guide explained a funeral was underway and disappeared down the corridor of the tribe's long house. I was left with the tribal mourners on their straw mats passing around what I guessed to be the customary Iban funeral moonshine. I handed the jar back to the chief and waited for the effects of the fluid to wash away my trepidation about being the only foreigner attending the service. I felt like the fifth wheel on a very important date.

It was absurdly hot. The Iban were all dressed in shorts, traditional underwear-like garb, and the woman had only tops on. Everyone was drinking and a few groups played a dice game I didn't recognize. I towered over them at six-foot-one. They were all a foot or two shorter and this difference was the source for some of the fascinated stares in my direction. Once some time passed and it became clear I may well be alone without my interpreter for a while — and not wanting to communicate solely through the passage of the jar —conversation became the primary goal. Not being able to speak the language, I resulted to drawing things in the dirt near the mat. I drew a few pictures, got some messages about airplanes across, and that was about it.

Perhaps it's human nature, or just a reflex of ours, the way we feel we must say something to fill the space, especially among strangers in close confines. The silence, there among the Iban in their traditional hut, felt as loud to me as a jet engine but once I accepted it, my curiosity gave way to the deceased villager who I'd never meet on my visit. What were they like? Were they funny? Did they have a family? How'd they walk? What did they want out of life?

Somewhere in this silent inquisition I found my brother. Borneo vanished. The tribe and their moonshine fell into the background. My attention was entirely on my eldest brother — my parents first child — who decades earlier had been murdered.

We don't know the specifics of how he died. He was an airborne ranger, stationed near Savannah Georgia. Earlier in his life he thought he might become a priest but he liked women too much for all that. He was a good-looking guy too, an all-American football player. He'd called us at home that Sunday before he died, having gone sailing for the day at a place no more than fifteen minutes from his bunk. His whole platoon was set to take part in Operation Urgent Fury — the U.S. invasion of the Caribbean island nation of Grenada to stop the spread of communism. Some shrimpers found his body on the side of the road the next morning, shot in the head.

I sat there in that Iban longhouse and thought about him. I thought about how his death felt, the way it broke my mother, the way it broke me. My heart was gone. All I felt I had left was my career and traveling. I felt I had to go and see all the places he wasn't able, for the both of us. In the ensuing years I was terrified, not of death, but of leading the wrong kind of life — a kind that would disappoint or not make up for the loss of my brother. I was scared I'd meet some girl, get her pregnant, and wind up working at the local shoe store at the mall. That fear threatened to cripple me and it revisited me there on the mat in Borneo.

Of course, I had been to funerals before. At that point, I'd lost my mother and another sibling — my twin brother — but I'd never been to a funeral abroad. Somehow, even the funerals I had been to at home felt as though they had been so packed with to-dos and people to greet and administrative tasks to shuffle around and take care of, that they passed by in a blur of emotion and exhaustion. I hardly experienced their funerals in any kind of visceral way. The silence in the Iban hut made me feel as though I was going through all their departures, the mysteries and the sorrows, more acutely than I had when their funerals had taken place.

If the curiosity of connections, adventure, and my spiritual-seeking were what first sent me abroad, the deaths of my family members kept me there. I wanted to keep running. Stopping felt too painful, too real. If I kept traveling, it was as if I could somehow keep them alive, even if they were just ghosts that could accompany me wherever I escaped to.

I was finally brought back to the present when the Iban chief and a few of the men started laughing. At first, I was worried they were laughing at me. I thought my face may have turned red from the alcohol or the heat, but as I assessed the situation, the older and younger men bubbling with laughter, it was clear they were laughing about the deceased.

Maybe they had been funny in general. Maybe they'd just done something funny once and someone had mentioned it. Maybe the tribespeople just wanted to laugh with death so near their doorstep. Not having an interpreter there I was left entirely to make my own meaning from the moment at hand. I took the opportunity, as I could when I was at my best-traveling-self, and looked at the bright side of death.

Maybe the dead can look down on us and maybe they can't. Maybe I was running away from something or maybe I was running toward it. Maybe going far helped me get a little closer to that missing piece of myself that I'd lost when my brother was killed. I took the opportunity then, and joined the Iban's chorus of laughter.

I'm getting my heart back slowly. I get it from the places I've been, from the people I met. People in the Western world always want more and more. They are not satisfied with what they have. I have seen people who are happier than a lark who have nothing. They don't know the outside world. They don't know technology. They don't have the basic comforts like a radiator, a stove, or a bathtub. They don't have any of that so they find happiness within themselves. That is what traveling does for me. Whenever I am feeling sorry for myself, or for what I've lost — whether it be a family member or a job or a moment — I look back at the places I've been and feel lucky to have had a roof over my head and food in my mouth. Travel is a good educator. It helps you get your head straight.

The funeral proper ended soon thereafter, the jar of moonshine having long been depleted, along with the balance of our laughter and pain. Later, dinner was served in the same bowls-of-simple-food-on-the-floor-style I'd grown accustomed to when I'd eaten amongst so many other indigenous tribes I'd visited in my many, many journeys. That night I was privileged to witness traditional dances where the Iban's masterful handiwork was on display in the headdresses for both men and women, which I imagined were fanciful crowns Iban angels might wear in heaven.

Letting Go in Phuket

"Move a little more to the left," I heard, as a family bumped into me.

"Sorry," I said, shuffling in the shin-high, soupy-warm water.

I had been gazing out at the narrow rock jutting out from the gentle lapping ocean waters. A few trees dotted the object and many more spread out in swaths of jungle on the sea cliffs beyond them. I take my fair share of photos but when I visit sights as beautiful as the one in front of me, I generally get a good long look with my own eyes first, as if I were in a museum studying a painting.

Once I felt I was clear of the group, I expected to hear some sort of apology but none was forthcoming. It's generally accepted as a courtesy to get out of the way for someone's photo opportunity but not for those of us who prefer to observe the artworks of the physical world without a lens in the way.

"One, two, three," the person with the camera counted. "Say James Bond!"

For many, any vision of paradise is incomplete without a white sandy beach and translucent waters. That holds doubly as true for tourists as it does for film producers. With so many iconic movie scenes taking place at these serene locals, it's no wonder that the locations where they are shot become twice as famous as both a real-world and silver screen paradise. Perhaps no place in the world fulfills both definitions of this category as perfectly as the aptly named James Bond Island at Khao Phing Kan's Phang Nga Bay, near Thailand's larger Phuket Island.

In the scene, from the 1974 film *The Man with the Golden Gun*, James Bond — played by Roger Moore — prepares to have a duel only to turn around and find the villain has vanished. For the film writers, this is merely a twist to get the audience scooting ever further to the edge of their seats. For travelers, however, unexpected twists like these in their vacation stories are unwelcome and can often resort in the whole affair going down in flames. Even if most people will recognize the frequency with which the world can put bumps in your road, there is a feeling of great injustice when these inconveniences visit someone on vacation.

Often, such inconveniences occur when we get to the major tourist sites — where stress is already at a high level. James Bond Island was one of those places for me and it wasn't because a few groups of people told me to move out of the way for their photo. It was because after two nights sleeping on a nearby island, I stood out on the sand where the seaplane was supposed to arrive to pick me up, and realized they were not going to come.

My days in Thailand had been spectacular. The main reason I'd visited the region was for its renowned kayaking. From sunup to sundown, I'd paddled in and out of many inlets and isles that dotted the area surrounding James Bond Island. The views were stunning, the water was perfect, and the whole experience had exceeded any expectations I had. Even the unexpected creatures I found in one cave I lucked upon added a sense of wonder to the trip.

When I coaxed the bow of my small vessel into the narrow opening of one sea cave, I had to wait for my eyes to adjust to the light in the enclosure. Once they did, a chill crept onto my skin and it wasn't just because of the lower temperature inside. Dozens of giant furry droplets hung suspended above me.

Oh shit.

Bats scare me. I'm not one of those people who can see the winged rodents flutter around overhead and shrug their shoulders. I take cover.

The sight sent me wobbling back and forth in my kayak like a cartoon character who shakes out of their shoes at the sight of a ghost. A few seconds later, the shaking took a violent turn and in trying to overcorrect, I sent myself flying overboard. Underwater I cursed myself and held my breath for as long as I could, hoping whatever bats were aflutter above could have the chance to resettle.

Ever so carefully, I poked my head back above water, gasping silently for air. Then, I slowly pulled myself back into my kayak and held my breath for fear that if my foolish splashing wasn't enough to wake the bats, maybe a whimper or grunt would be. By the time I was able to navigate out of the cave and back into the day's golden sun, I busted out laughing in the face of the danger narrowly avoided. I was so hysterical about the unexpected adventure, I balanced my paddle on the boat and gave myself a minute for the giggles to pass.

I'd stayed on a nearby isolated island with only a handful of huts. A local family took care of the hospitality there, making sure guests like me were well looked after, giving the whole experience a kind-of bed-and-breakfast-on-the-beach feel. They served up some of the most remarkable food I'd enjoyed during my many visits to the country. One night, while I sat with my toes dug into the sand looking up at a crystal-clear starry sky, the hosts brought over a sizeable red snapper they'd grilled with sea salt, then doused in a tamarind sauce with chunks of bell peppers, cilantro, limes, peanuts, and those unmistakable Thai chilies.

I couldn't communicate with the family's toddler. He was fascinated with me and followed me around the island one morning. Before too long I discovered he knew how to play rock-paper-scissors and that became our way of communicating. The two of us made the twenty-minute journey around the island's few hundred yards of circumference.

It was the sort of innocent, natural travel relationship you form when you don't have a care in the world. Yet, the morning of my scheduled departure, as I stood on the same section of the island where we'd played a carefree round of rock-paper-scissors no less than 24-hours earlier, the whole place suddenly took on an unappealing tint, the kind that happens to the world when you get broken up with.

This is, I thought at the time, *unbelievable*.

I had triple-checked with the company who flew the seaplane flights to Bangkok because I needed to make a connection there to return to the United States for an important work meeting. It wasn't one of those kinds of meetings where you could make a call and have it pushed back. It wasn't a meeting where they wouldn't notice I wasn't there. It was the kind of meeting my career depended on. Now, it looked like there was no way I was going to make it.

For the twenty minutes following the seaplane passing its first full hour of tardiness, I freaked out. I cursed my all-in adventurous spirit. *Why did I have to push my luck and squeeze the most of my vacation days? Why couldn't I just fly back with an extra buffer-day like normal people?* I cursed my job. *Why did I have a job which only gave me so few vacation days?* I even cursed the paradisiac strip of earth where I stood. *Why did I choose this logistically difficult setting for my last days in Thailand?*

In my frustration, I began pacing around the small island. Without really thinking about it, I walked all the way back to the site of James Bond Island. It was early in the morning, before any of the tourist boats had arrived. There weren't throngs of people taking photos. I had a chance to stand there and admire the curious, gorgeous painting the sea and rocks had carved for my pleasure.

It dazzled me and I decided that no matter what happened, I'd never regret making time to witness the spectacular. Almost on cue, the plane arrived not long after and I made it back for my meeting just fine.

When we're home, everything is familiar. We get lulled into a false sense of comfort where everything is under our control. The reality is that misfortune can visit us whether we are coming home from a routine shift at work or on a well-earned, pricey vacation in the middle of paradise. In the day-to-day duel between our agency and the unreadability of the greater world, my visit to James Bond Island taught me a lesson in self-awareness that recasts unforeseen changes in schedule as just another twist in the movie that is our life. When looked at right, they should only serve to make the greater story more enjoyable.

Discovering in Austria

She was sitting down outside of her small house in the tiny mountain town when we arrived. A scarf was wrapped around her head to fend off the afternoon breeze. Her skin beneath it was wrinkly. When she stood up, I saw she had an apron on over her heavyset figure. As she — the quintessential image of an aging European woman — waved us over, I gulped and readied myself for a conversation that, one way or another, was going to change my life.

At the time, I was working on my Hospitality & Tourism doctorate at Virginia Tech University. My dean had recommended I spend a year abroad teaching hotel management. When a boarding school in Switzerland was brought up, it was hard to turn the offer down. The Swiss alps had always fascinated me with their seemingly endless expanses, not to mention the reputation for exquisite cheeses and high caliber service. Yet, I felt drawn to the region for another reason too.

My great grandfather Dramberger came to America from nearby Austria in the late 1880s. Growing up in a small mountain town, he developed a strong sense of adventure from an early age and was always curious about the world outside the canyons he called home. Once he was of age, he decided to take a job on the European trains, hoping to see as many countries as he could.

When he was working the train from Budapest to Vienna, he met his first wife. She was Hungarian. Not long after, they married and decided they wanted to have a family. He didn't feel his job on the train was going to be enough if he had other mouths to feed. After much debate, he convinced his wife that there were better opportunities for them in America. He knew the government was giving land grants in places like Texas, which solved his money problems and appealed to the traveling, adventurous nature that led him to work on the trains in the first place.

At the time, crossing the Atlantic was no small feat. The couple knew there were risks inherent in the decision to go in the first place. Yet, when they got to Liverpool to board the ship to New York, they felt optimistic.

That enthusiasm was short lived. His wife got sick on the way, along with many other passengers. My great grandfather managed to stay healthy and did what he could to take care of her. Unfortunately, like many other women and children aboard, she wasn't strong enough to survive. By the time the boat docked in New York, she was dead.

As quick as he was able, my great grandfather left New York for San Antonio, where he discovered the rumored land grants were real. He got around sixty acres on a river and began his new life as a farmer. Not long after, a neighbor introduced my great grandfather to his young daughter, who would become my great grandmother. The two had a dozen kids.

Many years later, after they both died, one of their children — my grandaunt — traveled to Austria. She wanted to see where her father — my great grandfather Dramberger — was raised. The place was still inhabited by his siblings and their children. After their visit, she took home a photo of the small house in the tiny mountain town to Texas where I first saw it as a young boy.

I can't pretend the image of that house hadn't been at the forefront of my mind when I chose to spend my doctoral teaching year in nearby Switzerland. It wasn't as though I didn't have the opportunity to visit when I'd come to Europe before. In my younger years as a backpacker, I could have ventured over to see the small house and have that special experience of tracing your lineage. However, as a young person, I had other priorities and suspected that sort of visit could wait until I was older. As I entered the final phase of my PhD, I was entering those years between youth and middle age where your priorities shift and curiosity about where you came from gets the better of you. After all, it's necessary information if you want to know where you're going.

I knew I would make the trek to Austria at some point but the first opportunity I had to leave Switzerland, the nearby temptation on the other border — the one shared with Italy — was far too great to ignore. I wanted wine. I wanted pasta. I wanted all those things Switzerland was not.

Having already traveled throughout Italy before, I decided to ditch the traditional tourist towns and headed for Trieste. A mellow, medium sized port city sitting between Slovenia and the Adriatic Sea, Trieste was the perfect choice. There was classic Roman architecture, the ocean, and amazing food.

Because the city was the main port during the Austro-Hungarian empire, *Gulasch alla Triestina* was the one dish I couldn't miss trying. I found it on my first afternoon in town after the overnight train. One of the national dishes of Hungary, Goulash is a stew with meat, vegetables and a healthy helping of paprika. The Trieste version came complete with an enormous pile of tomato sauce on top. The whole concoction was a delicious and filling lunch after a long night on the train.

Inadvertently, the dish also brought my great-grandfather to mind. I wondered if he'd ever tried it on his own during the train rides from Austria to Hungary. I continued to think about him as I wondered down the town's charming streets later that afternoon and plopped down at a café for an espresso.

The only other patron at the small establishment was a local man who approached me after some time and asked in perfect English where I was from. He was my favorite kind of European local, unbothered by the throngs of Americans who came to his country and didn't speak the language, instead focusing on what he could learn from the travelers and finding out about their story.

Before long I found he was an expert on getting stories out of people and I told him my great-grandfather's. He asked when I was planning to go find his home and I paused for a moment. I wasn't sure.

"It's not my style to plan too far in advance," I said.

"Perfect," he said. "Let's go now."

As much of a by-the-seat-of-my-pants as I consider myself, the proposition took me completely off guard. All the same, no more than an hour later, I had checked out of my hotel and the two of us barreled up the highway in his car toward Austria.

A few hours later and two generations after my grandaunt's visit, I approached my ancestral home. While I knew it was impossible for her to be "expecting me" in the proper sense of the phrase, I also knew my grandaunt had written the Dramberger family a letter announcing I would be visiting at some point over the next year. The way she beckoned us up to the house made me feel like the letter must have been fresh in her mind. I was sure of it when the first words came out of her mouth.

"Guadalupe," she said. "Texas."

After that, she'd completely exhausted her English skills. Yet it was enough for me to discern beyond a reasonable doubt that she was, in fact, a real-life, European relative of mine. My great-grandfather's land was in Guadalupe County Texas, named after the thin Guadalupe river that snaked through the region near San Antonio, like the Dramberger blood did through my veins, leading me to that moment.

We were invited inside. A few other relatives emerged from the rooms of the humble home. As if it were written this way, one of them slid a bottle of Jägermeister on the table and said one word.

"Drink."

It was a direction I wasn't about to decline. Neither did my new Italian friend who was seeming to have as good of a time as I was on this impromptu quest to find out my origin story. We drank. We laughed. They spoke in broken phrases about my great-grandfather and my grandaunt. We ate lunch with my cousins. Afterward, we took a walk to the town cemetery where many other relatives were buried, all under a name that was slightly different than I expected: Tramburger.

There was something fitting that I travelled all that way to discover my real name was spelled different than I'd always known it. Like so many immigrants to the United States, the register spelled the name wrong and I felt good to be included among them. I felt grounded. I was thrilled I had taken my Italian friend up on this sudden, connective-spiritual-adventure and once our visit was over, I headed home to Switzerland on the train feeling like I never knew myself better.

Alone in the Maldives

My face was smashed into the soft cotton of a curved towel. My feet hung a foot and a half off the table. My arms dangled below, my fingertips just beyond the glass floor where I watched vibrant fish squiggle against the porcelain-colored sand and zip through pieces of coral reef.

Against my back, I felt two pairs of warm, worn hands, nearly depleted of the oils and lotions that had been deposited on my skin when I first laid down almost two hours earlier. When they'd finally finished, rainwater from the morning's storm that had been captured in a wood gutter on the roof and funneled down into the serene massage room was splashed in sections against my body. The oils and scents were washed away. Then the hands also disappeared, being replaced by a set of smooth, heated stones, their curves resting against each of my spine's segments.

I was alone — in the best sense of the word.

There were no meetings coming later that day. Nor were there any responsibilities during the handful of days prior or the next ones ahead. There was no phone or computer within reach. Apart from the masseuses, some sparse guests, and those who worked at the restaurant at the opposite end of the dock structure, I was all by myself.

It was disjointing at first, being so alone. I flew into Malé, the country's tightly packed capital city. By no means a megalopolis at just over 100,000 inhabitants, it is still flush with activity in the Maldives primary two industries of fishing and tourism. I had come to explore the latter and to take a break from recent people-adventure-spiritual-heavy itineraries. I had planned and prepared myself for the week alone but I wasn't ready for how spectacularly strange it was to truly be on my own without a thing to do or a place to go.

From Malé, I boarded a small rotary plane and crept briskly but briefly into the sky. The nation's many tiny islands dotted the liquid plain of turquoise below. The aircraft was up and then it was down faster than I could get my bearings. Once on the water, we meandered over to a dock.

The pilot tossed out my duffle bag, helped me leap from the plane to the dock, and said, "Pick you up in a week."

Then, he left.

As instructed, I waited on the dock. I was staggeringly alone. In the distance, I saw a few boats moving around, the same went for other small planes overhead. These objects took the shape of fuzzy dots rather than any discernable shapes. They might as well have been mirages and I might as well have been lost in a sea desert.

I had visited many island destinations in my life. Many were impressive. A few were rapturous but as I sat on the silent dock, I realized I had never been as alone as I was right then.

I imagined, for a moment, what my life might have been like had I taken a different path. I knew happy couples and unhappy ones. I had friends with children and those without. There were family members and friends of mine who had chosen high-powered, stressful careers that gave them so much money but so little time. I knew people on all sides of these divides who would give anything to be on the other side — to have the relationship they thought would complete them or be the reliable parent they never had. Seemingly everyone I'd come across was desperate for more: more money, more love, more friends, or more vacation time.

I'd felt some of these feelings in my life too. Whether I was on the road or off it, there had been moments where I gazed across at another lawn — even an imagined one — and deeply wished I had chosen differently. Perhaps it's human nature to want what we cannot have. In the end though, we live the life we choose. By definition, that choice eliminates some possibilities.

It is in those unchosen possibilities where people usually hide the biggest fears and regrets. It is there, when thinking of what they don't have, that they can feel the fiercest pains of loneliness. Though I'd felt them in the past, as I waited all by myself in what was an outer-space of ocean, I did not feel those pains.

I was alone but I was not lonely.

It felt like an eternity had passed when the small wooden boat finally skimmed to a stop at the dock that had become my temporary home. I hopped aboard. About fifteen minutes later I got off again and approached the small complex of wooden bungalows raised high off the water on support beams.

Over the next few days, I sank further into aloneness. I leapt from my suspended balcony into the warm seawater. I lounged in the sleepy hammocks. I read books I loved and wrote in my dairies about my own experiences.

I dined on opulent helpings of Maldivian cuisine, munching on savory *hedhikaa* snacks of fried, breaded meats and swept up lumps of the delicious mixture of *mas huni* — featuring minced tuna, onion, coconut, and chili with — with roshi bread. Freshly caught fish was always available to be caught and cooked by request, right in front of my eyes.

The hospitality industry in the Maldives was everything I'd been led to believe. The accommodation was top notch. The food was immaculate. The courtesy and politeness of the staff was second to none. A few decades earlier, it had been a country desperate to diversify its economy, its industry, and bring people to visit its incredible islands. The Maldives was an example of what a great tourism industry can do for a county, and climate change aside, the hospitality future for the small nation looked as bright as the sun when it shone down on the crystalized waters.

As I strolled back down the dock's walkway, the water gently lapping against the wooden walkway's stilts, I felt as though I was floating — high off the massage, the hospitality, and the travel experience. Best of all, I still had a few days of it to come. I was smack-dab in the middle of an immersive aloneness that, at the rate I was going, felt like it would lead to enlightenment. When I reached my quaint bungalow, I opened the door and stepped inside.

A delectable-looking fruit basket — featuring a rainbow of tropical colors I was more accustomed to seeing inside the bowl of sugary, artificially flavored children's cereals — rested gently on the coffee table in the room's small sitting area. Without a second thought, I snatched up one of the colorful morsels in one motion and slid my teeth through the squishy outer husk and gnawed on the meaty core. It was a custardy. It was slimy. It was disgusting.

My nose caught up with my taste buds — it was durian.

I'd smelled durian before, that rank, stewed, sock-like smell that tunnels unwelcomely into your nose the way a gopher does a golf course. I'd seen it stacked in its spikey, infant-sized, yellow-green entirety in front of markets across tropical Asia. The piles of durian — which is as loved and hated across the region as a divisive political leader — are forbidden from intermingling with the other foods for fear of their being toxified by its unmistakable stench. That smell can be detected even before the weapon of choice — often a machete — is hurled down upon its spiny exterior, revealing the creamy gold fruit pods lumped snugly inside. Once its open, there is no mistaking the smell.

It all made me wonder, how, exactly, these tourism experts, with their well-earned reputation, managed both the mistake of putting such a controversial snack amidst the confection as well as conjure the sorcery required to mask the smell. I wasn't floating ever so slightly off the earth any longer. I was completely out of orbit.

I slunk down onto the sofa and chuckled about everything at once. As I laughed, the moon hung low outside over the calm Maldivian waters. As well traveled as I was and as much as I felt I knew about tourism, being away — just as being alive — means there is always a trick up someone's sleeve. Better to be delighted by the surprises along the way than trying to convince yourself that — even when the elements are familiar — it's a show you've already seen. You'll only be unmoored by every reinterpretation.

Epilogue: Shangri-La of the Soul

To me, a destination is anywhere that demands full use of all five senses. I know what you're thinking: *Edward, I use all five of my senses every moment of every day.* But you don't. Not really.

To use all five of your senses, you must be out of your comfort zone. For most of us, when we're at home, we put things on autopilot. We're not on our toes. We're not present. We aren't using our five senses, except maybe passively.

You must breathe a destination. You must taste it and smell it and hear it. You must feel it — and live it.

Do you have to be far from home for this to happen?

There are New Yorkers who have never visited the Statue of Liberty but have flown to the pyramids in Egypt. There are those of us who drive by the little hole in the wall restaurant down the street every day without ever stopping to try it. The well-traveled are more susceptible to these kinds of traps but everyone in their daily routine has experienced it on some level.

What matters isn't the distance or duration separating you from your destination — it's whether the environment you create for it is conducive. Whether we travel for connection, adventure, spirit, self, or something else, we should cultivate an active role in our destination seeking if we want to travel *for* life and not *despite* it. As humans, we have some basic urge to see just around the horizon. We always think the grass is greener elsewhere. We believe utopia is there to be found. We assume that Shangri La, is just around the corner, we just have to get there first.

If we turn off autopilot and open-up our senses, how do we know the Shangri-La wouldn't simply appear, wherever we are, as though it was in our soul all along?